first 5

Printed in Canada by Hemlock Printers

Contact: contact@first15.org
www.first15.org

Designed by Matt Ravenelle
mattravenelle.com

ABOUT FIRST15

Spending time alone with God every day can be a struggle. We're busier – and more stressed – than ever. But still, we know it's important to spend time alone with our Creator. We know we need to read his word, pray, and worship him.

First15 bridges the gap between desire and reality, helping you establish the rhythm of meaningful, daily experiences in God's presence. First15 answers the critical questions:

• Why should I spend time alone with God?
• How do I spend time alone with God?
• How do I get the most out of my time alone with God?
• How can I become more consistent with my time alone with God?

And by answering these questions through the format of daily devotionals, you'll practice the rhythm of meeting with God while experiencing the incredible gift of his loving presence given to those who make time to meet with him.

Allow God's passionate pursuit to draw you in across the next several days. And watch as every day is better than the last as your life is built on the solid foundation of God's love through the power of consistent, meaningful time alone with him.

To learn more about First15, visit our website first15.org. First15 is available across mobile app, email, podcast, and our website. Subscribe to our devotional today and experience God in a fresh way every day.

ABOUT THE AUTHOR

Craig Denison is the author of First15, a daily devotional guiding over a million believers into a fresh experience with God every day. In 2015, Craig founded First15 after sensing a longing in God's heart for his people to be about relationship – real, restored relationship with him – that above all else, he simply wanted the hearts of his people. Craig began praying, dreaming, and writing. And the idea of helping people spend the first fifteen minutes of their day focusing on nothing else but growing in their relationship with God was born. The vision was birthed in Craig's heart that if we as a people would worship, read, and pray at the beginning of every day, everything could change for the better. Craig writes, speaks, and he and his wife, Rachel lead worship to help believers establish a more tangible, meaningful connection with God.

———————

CONTENTS

Stirring affections

01

WEEK

*"Bless the Lord, O my soul,
and all that is within me, bless
his holy name!" Psalm 103:1*

WEEKLY OVERVIEW

This week we'll spend time stirring up our affections for God through the renewing of our minds. Your mind is the gateway to your affections. What you think is worthy of your affections is what will receive them. So, as we grow in our understanding of God's overwhelming goodness we will naturally give him our hearts. May you be stirred by the unconditional love of your heavenly Father this week as his perfect nature is revealed to you in greater, more transformative ways.

The Sweetness of God's Love

DAY 1

DEVOTIONAL

Think about the death of Jesus for a moment. Picture how horrific the scene would have been to witness in person. Now try and imagine witnessing it from the Father's perspective. Think about how he saw, heard, felt, knew, and wept over everything that happened to Jesus. Think about how he felt placing the sin of the world, the sin of you and me, on the shoulders of his perfect and undeserving Son.

"And walk in love, as Christ loved us and gave himself up for us, a slain offering and sacrifice to God, a sweet fragrance."

EPHESIANS 5:2 AMP

I ask you to imagine all of that for one reason—to gain perspective on the unfathomable love of God as expressed in Ephesians 5:2. Scripture says, *"walk in love, as Christ loved us and gave himself up for us, a slain offering and sacrifice to God, a sweet fragrance."* When I read that verse initially I skipped over a life changing phrase: *"a sweet fragrance."* With all the Father witnessed that day, with all the suffering Jesus faithfully endured, God still considers Jesus' death *"a sweet fragrance."* How is that possible? How could anyone consider the death of Jesus a sweet fragrance, let alone the Father?

Such is the incredible depth of God's love for us that he would count the atrocities committed against his Son as a sweet fragrance. Such is the enormity of God's desire for restored relationship with us that he would look upon the death of his Son with favorable remembrance.

I don't think we as God's children understand the joy our Father feels when we spend time with him. I don't think we understand the depth of his love that he would pay the highest price simply to have unhindered relationship with us again. While meditating on this Scripture I realized I had never once thought about how tirelessly God has been working since Adam and Eve sinned simply to be able to enjoy his people again—to walk with them as he once had.

The death of Jesus was a turning point in the scope of eternity. His sacrifice meant a change from all of humanity opposing God to the crown of his creation returning to his fold. When God placed the sin of humanity on Christ's shoulders he was able to take the position of the father in the story of the prodigal son, running out to meet us as we are—his children finally able to return home to him for good.

God so longed for communion with you that he paid the ultimate price. He counts you worthy of the death of his Son. Let that truth shape your identity. Let God's love be the foundation for your perspective, thoughts, emotions and actions today. May your heart be stirred to live in light of God's unconditional love. May you be rooted in the unshakable nature of your heavenly Father. And may you live today in the eternal embrace of God, knowing that you are wholly and forever his beloved.

13

GUIDED PRAYER

1. Meditate on the sacrifice of Jesus. Allow Scripture to form a foundation of unconditional love for your heart.

"For Christ also suffered once for sins, the righteous for the unrighteous, that he might bring us to God." 1 Peter 3:18

"He entered once for all into the holy places, not by means of the blood of goats and calves but by means of his own blood, thus securing an eternal redemption." Hebrews 9:12

2. Meditate on who you are as a child of God. Form your identity around the truth of Scripture.

"But to all who did receive him, who believed in his name, he gave the right to become children of God." John 1:12

"But you are a chosen race, a royal priesthood, a holy nation, a people for his own possession, that you may proclaim the excellencies of him who called you out of darkness into his marvelous light. Once you were not a people, but now you are God's people; once you had not received mercy, but now you have received mercy." 1 Peter 2:9-10

3. Ask God to reveal the depth of his love for you. Rest in the reality of his nearness. Let him fill your heart with his love to overflowing.

"So that Christ may dwell in your hearts through faith—that you, being rooted and grounded in love, may have strength to comprehend with all the saints what is the breadth and length and height and depth, and to know the love of Christ that surpasses knowledge, that you may be filled with all the fullness of God." Ephesians 3:17-19

"So we have come to know and to believe the love that God has for us. God is love, and whoever abides in love abides in God, and God abides in him." 1 John 4:16

Don't let the opinion of others sway you from your firm foundation of God's love. What is the opinion of man in comparison to the perspective of God? If God counts relationship with you worth the death of Jesus, you are that valuable. Cast aside the fickle thoughts of others for the truthful, life-giving love of your heavenly Father. Rest in his presence and find hope and security in the truth that his arms are always open to you—ready to embrace you just as you are.

Extended Reading: 1 Peter 2

The Lord Your God is in Your Midst

DAY 2

DEVOTIONAL

Hardly a verse in all of Scripture sums up the heart of God for his people better than Zephaniah 3:17. As we walk through this passage today I pray your life would be transformed by the reality of God's nearness and the depth of his love for you. Scripture says,

The Lord your God is in your midst, a mighty one who will save; he will rejoice over you with gladness; he will quiet you by his love; he will exult over you with loud singing.

"The Lord your God is in your midst, a mighty one who will save; he will rejoice over you with gladness; he will quiet you by his love; he will exult over you with loud singing."

ZEPHANIAH 3:17

"God is in your midst"—take a moment to consider that fact. God is not far off; in fact, he is with you right now. If you are a Christian, his Spirit dwells within you, fellowshipping with your spirit. Psalm 139:7 says, *"Where shall I go from your Spirit? Or where shall I flee from your presence?"* God's presence is with you right now. He is in your midst.

He is *"a mighty one who will save."* As a believer you have been saved not of your own accord, but by the humble, loving sacrifice of Jesus. If you have confessed your faith in Christ, you are his forever and nothing can take away your salvation. Rejoice in him today; the Almighty God has come for you, and you now have nothing to fear. Salvation is yours in him; you are a child of God.

"He will rejoice over you with gladness." To rejoice over you means to rejoice in who you are. Do you believe that God rejoices in who you are? The world is in the business of convincing you that you're nothing to rejoice about. Your enemy constantly points out things you do wrong, attempting to convince you that you aren't lovable—that you are worthless. But the Bible says that God will rejoice over you with gladness. God believes that you are worth the death of his Son, and there is nothing you can do to change his mind. He rejoices over you today.

"He will quiet you with his love." How often do you allow God to do this? How often do you take time to let him quiet your life with his love? This is his promise, but like any other gift it has to be received. His desire is to bring a quiet peace to the stress and worry of your world. You have God's peace available to you any time you are willing to surrender your heart and be filled with his presence.

"He will exult over you with loud singing." To exult over you means to show or feel elation or jubilation, as the result of a success. Do you know that God sees you as a success? The story of Scripture is God creating mankind for the purpose of having communion and fellowship with us. He lost that perfect communion when mankind chose sin over him, and he has been working to restore it ever since. With the death of Jesus, the curse is broken, our sin is paid for, and we are now able to walk in restored relationship with God. God now has what he has longed for all this time—you. He exults over you because there is nothing between you and him. To God simply having relationship with you makes you a success already.

As a believer you can live out of the great victory God has achieved in you. You get to meet with God face to face. God is present with you today, desiring to do all that Zephaniah 3:17 promises. Allow God to come and fulfill his promises in your life as you enter into guided prayer.

GUIDED PRAYER

1. Receive God's presence by meditating on this truth: God is in your midst.

"The Lord your God is in your midst." Zephaniah 3:17

"My presence will go with you, and I will give you rest." Exodus 33:14

"Splendor and majesty are before him; strength and joy are in his place." 1 Chronicles 16:27

2. Receive the quiet heart that his love brings as you meditate on Scripture.

"He will quiet you by his love." Zephaniah 3:17

"But you, O Lord, are a God merciful and gracious, slow to anger and abounding in steadfast love and faithfulness." Psalm 86:15

"Give thanks to the God of heaven, for his steadfast love endures forever." Psalm 136:26

3. Allow the truth of Scripture to go deeper into your heart. Your Father rejoices over you with gladness. He exults over you with loud singing. You are a success in his eyes.

"He will rejoice over you with gladness." Zephaniah 3:17

"He will exult over you with loud singing." Zephaniah 3:17

"Let me see your face, let me hear your voice, for your voice is sweet, and your face is lovely." Song of Solomon 2:14

When the cares of the world come and crowd out the peace of God's presence, turn your attention toward him and receive what he has already promised to give you. Memorizing a verse like Zephaniah 3:17 will help you consistently experience the promises of God. Meditating on it throughout your day is the best gift you could give yourself today. Make some time to memorize Zephaniah 3:17 that it might become more than words on a page and produce transforming, transcendent peace and joy.

Extended Reading: Memorize Zephaniah 3:17

God our Father

DEVOTIONAL

As a follower of Jesus you have been brought into the family of God. Take a moment to let that truth sink in. Think about what it means to have God, the Creator of the universe, the embodiment of Perfect Love, as your Father. So often we lose sight of the fact that God is our Father and view him through perspectives not aligned with Scripture. We view God through lenses the world and unfortunate experiences have given us rather than a revelation of him as a good Father given to us by the revolutionary teaching of Jesus.

"See what kind of love the Father has given to us, that we should be called children of God; and so we are."

1 JOHN 3:1

In Matthew 7:9-11 Jesus teaches us, *"Which one of you, if his son asks him for bread, will give him a stone? Or if he asks for a fish, will give him a serpent? If you then, who are evil, know how to give good gifts to your children, how much more will your Father who is in heaven give good things to those who ask him!"* You have a Father who loves to give you good gifts. So often we think of God as a harsh disciplinarian who never lets his kids enjoy life. We assume he will say no to anything that gives us pleasure as if he only wanted us to go to church more, pray more, or give more time and money. But that's not the heart of your Father. Your God is the author of joy, pleasure, happiness, and good gifts. He longs for your life to be filled with the perfect gifts he has planned for you every day. John 10:10 says, *"I came that they may have life and have it abundantly."* As your perfect Shepherd, God will faithfully guide you to and supply you with all you need to live marked by fullness of life.

In Matthew 19:14, Jesus displays the heart of the Father when he says, *"Let the little children come to me and do not hinder them, for to such belongs the kingdom of heaven."*

As our Father, God longs for us as his children to simply be with him. He longs for us to know his love and embrace—to let it be the foundation of everything we do. More than God desires any task of you, he longs for your heart. So great was his desire for just the opportunity of relationship with you that Jesus displayed the fullness of God's unconditional love by willingly laying down his life for you. There is no room in Scripture to view God as anything but perfectly loving and good. View God as the good Father he is, and run to him with open arms and an open heart that you might find fullness of life in his eternal embrace.

Take time in guided prayer to allow God's presence to overcome misconceptions you might have about him. Often if we've been in church for long enough we stop at a theological understanding of God the Father and don't allow time and space for him to heal our hearts and transform our lives. Don't let that happen today! You have a good Father who loves and longs to simply meet with you. Spend time with him today getting lost in the sweetness of restored relationship.

GUIDED PRAYER

1. Receive God's presence as you meditate on Scripture.

"See what kind of love the Father has given to us, that we should be called children of God; and so we are." 1 John 3:1

"Let the little children come to me and do not hinder them, for to such belongs the kingdom of heaven." Matthew 19:14

2. Ask God how he feels about you. Listen and quiet your soul to receive a revelation of his heart.

"God loves each of us as if there were only one of us." Augustine

"Every good gift and every perfect gift is from above, coming down from the Father of lights with whom there is no variation or shadow due to change." James 1:17

3. Where do you need to apply God's character to your life? In what ways are you living as if God was a taskmaster rather than a good Father? In what ways are you seeking to provide for yourself rather than working to receive provision God has already promised?

"Which one of you, if his son asks him for bread, will give him a stone? Or if he asks for a fish, will give him a serpent? If you then, who are evil, know how to give good gifts to your children, how much more will your Father who is in heaven give good things to those who ask him!" Matthew 7:9-11

"Therefore do not be anxious, saying, 'What shall we eat?' or 'What shall we drink?' or 'What shall we wear?' For the Gentiles seek after all these things, and your heavenly Father knows that you need them all. But seek first the kingdom of God and his righteousness, and all these things will be added to you." Matthew 6:31-33

In every trial and circumstance you face today, God has a plan to lead you perfectly. He is not a God who sits back and watches as we try to figure life out. He wants to get involved in all that you do, just as a perfect father wants to help his children succeed and live with joy. Ask God what he thinks about what you're doing. If you run into a problem today, ask for the Spirit's guidance. Doing your day with God is the absolute best way to live. He knows everything and has a perfect plan for you! Take time today to listen to God and trust his leading.

Extended Reading: 1 John 3

Delighting in
God's Love

DAY 4

DEVOTIONAL

John 17 is an incredibly significant passage of Scripture for Christians today. Jesus prayed perfectly in accordance with the will of the Father, in submission to him during his time on earth. Therefore, everything Jesus prayed, God will accomplish. Part of the beauty of their oneness is shared desires. In John 17:26, Jesus prays to the Father, *"I made known to them your name, and I will continue to make it known, that the love with which you have loved me may be in them, and I in them."* Imagine

"I made known to them your name,
and I will continue to make it known,
that the love with which you have loved
me may be in them, and I in them."

JOHN 17:26

that! Jesus says we can have the same love in us with which God the Father loved Jesus. Think of the magnitude of love the Father has for his Son, and now think about God having that same magnitude of love for you! You are his beloved, his prized possession. Your heavenly Father gave up his own Son to have a personal relationship with you, to be able to pour his vast love out on you.

The Bible describes David as a man after God's own heart (Acts 13:22). He was a man who delighted in God's love and experienced the joy of his presence throughout various seasons of life. In Psalm 16:5-11 David wrote, *"The Lord is my chosen portion and my cup; you hold my lot. The lines have fallen for me in pleasant places; indeed, I have a beautiful inheritance. I bless the Lord who gives me counsel; in the night also my heart instructs me. I have set the Lord always before me; because he is at my right hand, I shall not be shaken. Therefore my heart is glad, and my whole being rejoices; my flesh also dwells secure. For you will not abandon my soul to Sheol, or let your holy one see corruption. You make known to me the path of life; in your presence there is fullness of joy; at your right hand are pleasures forevermore."* When I read David's words I can't help but desire his joy and security. I am filled with a desire to know that kind of love in my own life. Psalm 16 makes me desire to have God as *"my chosen portion,"* and I wholeheartedly want to experience *"pleasures forevermore."* What about you?

Allow your desires be stirred to experience for yourself the immeasurable love with which God has loved Jesus. Know that it's not only your desire to experience love, but the desire of your heavenly Father as well (John 17:26). In what areas of your life do you need to *"set the Lord always before"* you? What areas do you need him to be *"at [your] right hand?"* In the Lord, there truly are *"pleasures forevermore."*

Take time today to simply delight in your God, and allow his presence to flood the dry, weary places of your heart. You are his chosen portion, the apple of his eye. God gave up his only Son for the chance to meet with you right now. Simply open up your heart and delight in the love of your heavenly Father.

25

GUIDED PRAYER

1. Meditate on John 17:26. Allow Scripture to give you a better revelation of the depth of God's love for you.

"That the love with which you have loved me may be in them, and I in them." John 17:26

2. Where do you need to delight in the love of God today? Where is your life not marked by the fullness of joy David described in Psalm 16?

"In your presence there is fullness of joy; at your right hand are pleasures forevermore." Psalm 16:11

3. Now simply delight in the love of God for you, the very same love that he has for his Son, Jesus Christ.

"Delight yourself in the Lord, and he will give you the desires of your heart." Psalm 37:4

Every day is a battle to root yourself in the love of God. But it is a battle worth fighting. It's a battle waged within the depths of your soul—the fight between what God and the world says matters. When you make more space for God to fill by ridding yourself of the ways of the world, his heart and mind will become your own. What matters to him will begin to matter to you. Keeping his love in perspective will become as natural as breathing. The fullness of relationship with him is meant to be our source, portion, strength and desire. Give way to his loving kindness today, and let the cares of the world go in light of his goodness and grace.

Extended Reading: John 17

God Heals Hearts

DEVOTIONAL

One of my favorite chapters in all of Scripture is Psalm 147. It's a psalm laden with the wondrous works of God, rich with imagery and powerful in stirring our affections for God. In it we learn that God *"determines the number of the stars; he gives to all of them their names,"* and that he *"covers the heavens with clouds; he prepares rain for the earth; he makes grass grow on the hills. He gives to the beasts their food, and to the young ravens that cry."*

*"He heals the brokenhearted
and binds up their wounds."*

PSALM 147:3

The verse that I want to emphasize for us today, however, is verse 3: *"He heals the brokenhearted and binds up their wounds."* Jesus was a perfect example of God's heart to do this very thing. All throughout his ministry Jesus healed those around him physically, emotionally, and spiritually. Scripture gives us insight into characters such as Mary Magdalene, who was delivered of demon possession and brought into close friendship with Christ himself. Jesus healed her spiritually, emotionally, and physically by delivering her from oppression and being her friend. Then there's Paul. Before Jesus revealed himself to Paul, he was Saul, a man committed to destroying the very movement of Christianity that he would later give his life to build. He was a driven, successful, and prideful man. He was a religious zealot of great discipline, but a man far away from the heart of God. However, after meeting Jesus and being healed of his former ways, he was able to confidently say he counted all things *as loss because of the surpassing worth of knowing Christ Jesus my Lord. For his sake I have suffered the loss of all things and count them as rubbish, in order that I may gain Christ."*

God has the same heart for you he had for Mary and Paul. He knows the wounds that people, circumstances, and sin have caused in your life. He knows what you struggle with, the habits and addictions that hold you back from living the abundant life he has planned for you. And he has both a desire and plan to heal those wounds. God desires to heal your heart right now. You don't have to wait to encounter the power of God. God wants you to live a life receptive to all the love and blessing he longs to give you.

Let the stories of Mary and Paul fill you with a longing to encounter more of God. Allow what God has done in others' lives to stir up a yearning to be healed by God yourself. Wait on the Lord, open your heart to him, and let him do what he has promised to do in you. He's promised his healing, transformation, and abundant life. All that's left is for you to receive the gift of healing he longs to give as you follow the leading of the Holy Spirit today.

Take time to press into the heart of God to heal you today as you enter into a time of guided prayer.

GUIDED PRAYER

1. Meditate on God's desire to heal any broken places in your life as revealed in Scripture.

"He heals the brokenhearted and binds up their wounds." Psalm 147:3

"He himself bore our sins in his body on the tree, that we might die to sin and live to righteousness. By his wounds you have been healed." 1 Peter 2:24

"Bless the Lord, O my soul, and forget not all his benefits, who forgives all your iniquity, who heals all your diseases, who redeems your life from the pit, who crowns you with steadfast love and mercy." Psalm 103:2-4

2. Tell God of the places in your heart that are broken. Your wounds could go back to your childhood or just yesterday. Either way, God desires to heal anything that's holding you back from fullness of life in him.

"Heal me, O Lord, and I shall be healed; save me, and I shall be saved, for you are my praise." Jeremiah 17:14

3. Take action where God is leading you. Sometimes healing comes through forgiveness, a conversation, or taking some extra time to pray and be with God. Ask him how he feels about any wounds from your past, any broken relationships, or any recurring sin in your life. Journal what he says.

Healing is often a process, but know that God desires to lead you through every step of the way. If he puts it on your heart to forgive someone or to have a hard conversation, know that it's best for you. While it may be hard today, your life will be better because of it. Even if the person that hurt you has passed away, you can still forgive that person. As these issues begin to come up, take time to be in God's presence and allow him to heal the broken places in your life. God has healing and transformation in store for you, and that life is available to you right now.

Extended Reading: Psalm 147

The Heart of
God to Forgive

DEVOTIONAL

As much as God hates sin because of its destructive effects on us and others, he hates even more that something could come between our relationship with him. Because he desired a relationship with us, God sent his Son to pay the price for our restoration. And it's because of his continued love for us that he forgives us the very moment we repent of our sin. There's no price to pay. There's no time we have to spend outside of his perfect love. Jesus paid the price for every sin you and I will ever commit.

Think for a moment about your normal routine after you sin. What process do you usually go through before you feel restored to God? How long do you wait to repent? How much time do you usually let pass before you feel you can open your heart to God and enjoy him? It's true that the consequences of sin can linger even after we ask forgiveness, but an obstacle in our relationship with God is not one of them. Jesus paid the highest price, his own life, so that nothing could ever come between us and God again. The Bible says in Romans 8:33-39,

Who shall bring any charge against God's elect? It is God who justifies. Who is to condemn? Christ Jesus is the one who died—more than that, who was raised—who is at the right hand of God, who indeed is interceding for us. Who shall separate us from the love of Christ?

"If we confess our sins, he is faithful and just to forgive us our sins and to cleanse us from all unrighteousness."

1 JOHN 1:9

Shall tribulation, or distress, or persecution, or famine, or nakedness, or danger, or sword... For I am sure that neither death nor life, nor angels nor rulers, nor things present nor things to come, nor powers, nor height nor depth, nor anything else in all creation, will be able to separate us from the love of God in Christ Jesus our Lord.

The depth of God's unconditional love for you drives him to forgive you. Psalm 103:12 says, *"As far as the east is from the west, so far does he remove our transgressions from us."* After you confess your sin to him, he chooses to remember it no more. If you feel reminded of a transgression, it is not the voice of the Spirit. You have an enemy who lies constantly to form barriers between you and God. Because the enemy can no longer keep you from heaven, he will work tirelessly to wreck your relationship with God here on the earth. The moment you confess your sin to God is the moment there is nothing between you. Allow nothing to hinder your relationship with your heavenly Father. Renew your mind to the truth of what God says about your sin. God's heart is to forgive you now and forever. His heart is to lead you into perfect relationship with him every day, all day. Say yes to God's leading today, and rid yourself of the condemnation of past sins he has already forgotten.

GUIDED PRAYER

1. Let the peace of God which surpasses all understanding fill your room right now.

"Do not be anxious about anything, but in everything by prayer and supplication with thanksgiving let your requests be made known to God. And the peace of God, which surpasses all understanding, will guard your hearts and your minds in Christ Jesus." Philippians 4:6-7

2. Now ask God to reveal any sin in your life, and take some time for confession. Again remember that God's heart is not to condemn, but to heal. Write down your confession if it helps you focus or remember.

"He does not deal with us according to our sins, nor repay us according to our iniquities. For as high as the heavens are above the earth, so great is his steadfast love toward those who fear him; as far as the east is from the west, so far does he remove our transgressions from us. As a father shows compassion to his children, so the Lord shows compassion to those who fear him. For he knows our frame; he remembers that we are dust." Psalm 103:10-14

3. Receive his forgiveness for your sin. An incredibly important part of confession is receiving

forgiveness. Choose not to punish yourself any longer. Choose not to veil your heart before God because of shame. Align your heart with the truth that he chooses not to remember your sin after you confess.

"If we confess our sins, he is faithful and just to forgive us our sins and to cleanse us from all unrighteousness." 1 John 1:9

Restoration with God so often hinges upon our choices. Will you choose to condemn yourself? Will you choose to listen to the voice of your enemy who reminds you of past transgressions? Or will you choose to trust God at his word and receive total restoration with the Father? The choice you make will profoundly impact your quality of life. You were made for unhindered relationship with God. Anything that gets in the way of you and him needs to be removed as quickly as possible. Receive his forgiveness today. Whenever you are reminded of past sin, align your heart with God's word through the renewing of your mind. Live in restored relationship with your heavenly Father today.

Extended Reading: Romans 8

A Constant Companion

DAY 7

DEVOTIONAL

At salvation you were given the gift of God himself,
the Spirit of Christ, dwelling within you. Ephesians
1:13-14 says, *"In him you also, when you heard the word
of truth, the gospel of your salvation, and believed in him,
were sealed with the promised Holy Spirit, who is the
guarantee of our inheritance until we acquire possession
of it, to the praise of his glory."* And with the indwelling
of the Spirit, friendship with God has been made

"Likewise the Spirit helps us in our weakness. For we do not know what to pray for as we ought, but the Spirit himself intercedes for us with groanings too deep for words. And he who searches hearts knows what is the mind of the Spirit, because the Spirit intercedes for the saints according to the will of God."

ROMANS 8:26-27

available to greater depths than you can imagine. He longs to spend time with you like a friend. He longs for you to know how he feels, what he thinks is best and your heavenly Father's heart for you.

Scripture teaches us a lot about the character of the Spirit. Acts 13:2 teaches us that the Spirit speaks: *"While they were worshiping the Lord and fasting, the Holy Spirit said, 'Set apart for me Barnabas and Saul for the work to which I have called them.'"* In Ephesians 4:30 we learn that the Spirit feels emotions like grief: *"And do not grieve the Holy Spirit of God, by whom you were sealed for the day of redemption."* Romans 8:26-27 teaches us that the Spirit is our Helper and prays for us: *"Likewise the Spirit helps us in our weakness. For we do not know what to pray for as we ought, but the Spirit himself intercedes for us with groanings too deep for words. And he who searches hearts knows what is the mind of the Spirit, because the Spirit intercedes for the saints according to the will of God."* Friendship with the Spirit is one of God's greatest gifts to us. He speaks to us, is emotionally invested in our lives, helps us in our weakness and prays for us when we don't have the words.

So great is God's love for you that he sent his Spirit to dwell with you. So great is his desire for continued relationship with you that, in his grace, he has given you himself as a constant companion. Another important characteristic of the Spirit, however, is that he will not force relationship on you. He speaks when you listen, he gives you revelation as you open your mind to receive it, and he leads you as you ask for his guidance. The Spirit is full of incredible power but also incredible meekness and humility. He is both powerful and respectful. If you ask for a deeper friendship with the Holy Spirit, you will find he is the best friend you have ever known.

Take time as you enter into guided prayer to get to know the Holy Spirit like a friend. In his book *The Pursuit of God* A.W. Tozer writes, "Religion, so far as it is genuine, is in essence the response of created personalities to the creating personality, God." The Holy Spirit has a personality. He has likes and dislikes. He feels, thinks, enjoys, likes, suffers, and desires. May your time in prayer be filled with new levels of friendship with the Spirit of God dwelling within you.

GUIDED PRAYER

1. Ask the Holy Spirit to reveal his nearness to you. Take time to acknowledge his presence.

"In him you also, when you heard the word of truth, the gospel of your salvation, and believed in him, were sealed with the promised Holy Spirit, who is the guarantee of our inheritance until we acquire possession of it, to the praise of his glory." Ephesians 1:13-14

2. Give thanks to the Spirit for who he is. Thank him for his presence in your life. Thank him for his desire to speak to you, lead you, help you and pray for you. *"While they were worshiping the Lord and fasting, the Holy Spirit said, 'Set apart for me Barnabas and Saul for the work to which I have called them.'"* Acts 13:2

"Likewise the Spirit helps us in our weakness. For we do not know what to pray for as we ought, but the Spirit himself intercedes for us with groanings too deep for words. And he who searches hearts knows what is the mind of the Spirit, because the Spirit intercedes for the saints according to the will of God."* Romans 8:26-27

3. Now ask the Spirit how he's currently feeling. Ask him his perspective on anything in your life or the world around you. Listen and pay attention to any inclination you feel brought to mind. Journal what he says.

Friendship with the Spirit is like any other friendship in that it develops over time. Like a new friend, you must get to know his character and personality. Spend time just talking with him, listening to him and allowing him to work in your heart and life. He is an incredible gift given to you. He is your gateway to experiencing the things of God. Walk in relationship with him, follow his guidance, and make a new best friend in the Holy Spirit.

Extended Reading: Ephesians 1

Knowing God

" I will give them a heart to know that I am the Lord, and they shall be my people and I will be their God, for they shall return to me with their whole heart." Jeremiah 24:7

WEEKLY OVERVIEW

God has designed us to see him, to know his character, and to let the truth of his goodness lead us into deeper relationship with him. Augustine wrote, "Thou hast formed us for Thyself, and our hearts are restless till they find rest in Thee." In seeing God for who he is, our hearts are naturally stirred to find rest in his goodness. May your heart be stirred at the revelation of God's wonderful character.

Your Father Gives Good Gifts

DAY 8

DEVOTIONAL

One of my favorite parts of God's heart is his desire to give us amazing gifts. James 1:17 says, *"Every good gift and every perfect gift is from above, coming down from the Father of lights with whom there is no variation or shadow due to change."* Every good gift you receive is because God loves you. His love for you is so great that he looks for every opportunity to give you a gift. He desperately wants you to know that you are loved and valued by him. He so deeply wants you to know that he is not distant from you but, rather, is working in your midst to lead you to abundant joy, peace and life.

"Every good gift and every perfect gift is from above,
coming down from the Father of lights with whom
there is no variation or shadow due to change."

JAMES 1:17

Matthew 7:11 says, *"If you then, who are evil, know how to give good gifts to your children, how much more will your Father who is in heaven give good things to those who ask him!"* I love how God has chosen to be known to us as a Father. And because God has chosen to reveal himself as a Father, we can more tangibly understand the love of God by looking to good earthly parents. God longs to bless you the way a good Father would. And at the same time he loves you more deeply and powerfully than any earthly parent ever could. Our heavenly Father far outdoes any example an earthly father give us. What gift are you longing for today? Do you long for friendship? Do you need a greater sense of being loved? Do you just need to know that he is with you?

God's gifts may not look like a present you opened for Christmas last year, but they will be exactly what you need when you need it. If you need a friend, ask God for one! He's promised you his friendship, and he loves to guide his children into community with others. Do you need to know you're loved? God so longs for you to know the depth of his love that he sent his only Son to die for you! He'd love to pour his love out on you right now. Do you need to know that God is with you? Just ask for his manifest presence. Ask the Spirit to give you eyes to see all the ways he is working in your life. Ask God to reveal to you the ways he was, is and always will be with you. Do you need financial provision? Ask for the leading of the Holy Spirit in your finances! Ask God to provide for you what you need. Whatever gift you need from God today, his word promises in 1 John 5:15, *"if we know that he hears us in whatever we ask, we know that we have the requests that we have asked of him."* Your God hears you today. What's more, he will respond to you perfectly.

God's gifts are much more life-giving than anything an earthly parent could give. He gives the gift of a beautiful sunrise because he knows you have a longing to gaze upon beauty. He gives the gift of his presence because he knows you need the peace that only he can bring. He gives you the gift of friendship because he knows you aren't made to do life alone. He provides your finances because he cares about everything you need and desires to use you to bless others. Spend some time today reflecting on the amazing gifts he has given you. Thank him for his desire to bless you. Worship him because he is good. And open your heart to receive all the gifts your heavenly Father longs to give you today.

47

GUIDED PRAYER

1. Take a minute to reflect on all the good gifts you've been given by God.

2. Now thank God for everything you've been given. Thank him for your friends, family, job, church—anything that you love. Let thanksgiving stir your affections to know your heavenly Father more.

"Give thanks in all circumstances; for this is the will of God in Christ Jesus for you." 1 Thessalonians 5:18

3. Now ask the Spirit to open your eyes and heart to see and receive all the gifts God has in store for you today. Often to know a gift comes from God, we must be in tune with the Spirit. For a sunset to tell us of God's love, we must be sensitive to God's presence in our lives.

Thanking God for what he's already given us is a powerful way to position our hearts to be receptive to what he will give us in the future. Life is so much better when we acknowledge what God is doing in our midst. Knowing you are loved, liked and cared for is better than any material possession you could receive. You have a heavenly Father who gives amazing gifts. Celebrate his love today. And receive all that he longs to give you.

Extended Reading: Matthew 7

The Yoke of Jesus

DEVOTIONAL

Scripture describes a great exchange of our burdens for the peace of God. Jesus said in Matthew 11:28-30, *"Come to me, all who labor and are heavy laden, and I will give you rest. Take my yoke upon you, and learn from me, for I am gentle and lowly in heart, and you will find rest for your souls. For my yoke is easy, and my burden is light."* You have a God who loves you so much that he offers to take your burdens off your own shoulders, place them on his, and give you peace in return. Where does your life feel heavy? Where do you feel buried under the burdens of the world? God offers you his peace today if you will take some time to align yourself with him and *"yoke"* yourself to the teaching of Jesus.

In Matthew 11, Jesus presents us with an image of two animals sharing the burden of work together. The point Jesus is making here is in reference to coming under his teaching. He asks us, *"Take my yoke upon you, and learn from me, for I am gentle and lowly in heart, and you will find rest for your souls."* He isn't asking us simply to cast our burdens on him, but also to humble ourselves and submit to his teaching. If we are willing to come underneath him as our Teacher, then we no longer carry the burden of figuring out life on our own. And in freedom we are able to live life under the power and influence of the Holy Spirit.

Do you ever feel alone in what you're doing? Do you ever feel like peace is an unobtainable goal, blocked by layer upon layer of work you need to get through first? God's plan is different than the world's plan. The world says you can only have peace when you've completed the job, become

"Come to me, all who labor and are heavy laden, and I will give you rest. Take my yoke upon you, and learn from me, for I am gentle and lowly in heart, and you will find rest for your souls. For my yoke is easy, and my burden is light."

MATTHEW 11:28-30

the best, or gained the approval of man. God tells you to stop working in your own strength, yoke yourself to his teaching, and rid yourself of all the stress and pressure of the world. 1 Peter 5:7 says *"[Cast] all your anxieties on him, because he cares for you."* You have a God who cares about you. Your God is for you. He knows society tells you to work for and care about certain things, but he offers you the refuge of his peace instead.

You serve a God who doesn't want you to live even one day burdened. Every day, you can wake up and choose to yoke yourself to your heavenly Father and his word. Proverbs 3:5-6 says, *"Trust in the Lord with all your heart, and do not lean on your own understanding. In all your ways acknowledge him, and he will make straight your paths."* Align

your mind with what he says about you—casting off every opinion other than his. Align your day with the leading of God's Spirit, and receive the anointing and power he longs to bring into every situation.

God says, *"My yoke is easy, and my burden is light."* If you will choose God today over the way you've done things in the past, if you will choose to obey his word, then *"you will find rest for your souls."* What area of your life needs rest today? In what parts of your heart do you need God's peace and ease? He's waiting right now to meet with you, to offer you his yoke. Let him take your burdens, fears, and stress. Our fragile frame wasn't meant to bear such pressure. Come underneath God's teaching today, align your thinking with his, and let the cares of the world fall off as you live in light of the teaching of Jesus.

GUIDED PRAYER

1. Reflect on your life for a minute. In what areas do you need God's peace today? It could be your mindset, your appearance, friends, family, work, anything that you feel burdened by.

2. Now offer that area of your life to God and ask him for his opinion. Listen to God and let him tell you what he thinks about you. Look up verses that reveal his teaching on the subject.

3. Meditate on Scripture or what God spoke regarding the area in which you need peace. Let his peace flood that area of your life. Submit yourself to his word. Believe that he sees things truthfully. Whatever God says goes.

"Come to me, all who labor and are heavy laden, and I will give you rest. Take my yoke upon you, and learn from me, for I am gentle and lowly in heart, and you will find rest for your souls. For my yoke is easy, and my burden is light." Matthew 11:28-30

Yoke yourself to the teaching of Jesus today. Let his word be your refuge in a world full of opinions. Doing life yoked to God, being obedient to his word, is the best way to walk the path God lays out for us to abundant life. Every day attacks will come your way. But every day God has provided the truth you need in his word to fight those attacks. Choose the word of Jesus today, walk in obedience to it, and experience God's *"rest for your [soul]."*

Extended Reading: Matthew 11

The Boundless
Grace of God

DEVOTIONAL

Grace is one of the most astounding and life-transforming aspects of God's character. From the beginning of time God has chosen to lavish grace upon us instead of wrath. Time and time again, we've turned our backs on him. And time and time again he demonstrates the depth of his desire for us through the giving of his boundless grace. In his grace we are afforded a life not only apart from his wrath, but lived in the glory of relationship with our Creator through the redemption of Jesus.

"In him we have redemption through his blood, the forgiveness of our trespasses, according to the riches of his grace."

EPHESIANS 1:7

Ephesians 1:7 says, *"In him we have redemption through his blood, the forgiveness of our trespasses, according to the riches of his grace."* Let's look at a few of these ideas today and let them stir our affections for God. Allow God to speak through his word to the places of your heart where the grace of God hasn't been given the opportunity to abound yet.

Paul says that in Jesus we have *"redemption through his blood."* Have you thought about the nature of your redemption at length before? Colossians 1:19-22 says, *"For in him all the fullness of God was pleased to dwell, and through him to reconcile to himself all things, whether on earth or in heaven, making peace by the blood of his cross. And you, who once were alienated and hostile in mind, doing evil deeds, he has now reconciled in his body of flesh by his death, in order to present you holy and blameless and above reproach before him."* Such is the grace of your heavenly Father that there is not a single thing between you and him. You, who at one time stood apart from God, have been brought into the family of God, redeemed by the blood of Jesus.

Not only have you been redeemed once and for all, but you are forgiven both now and forever. Paul writes that we as believers have *"the forgiveness of our trespasses, according to the riches of his grace."* Where in your life do you need forgiveness today?

What do you feel is separating you from unveiled relationship with your heavenly Father? When you confess your sins, God offers you his forgiveness for anything you have done. *"According to the riches of his grace,"* which was made perfectly evident in the death of Jesus, you are being offered forgiveness. If God would send his Son to die in order to have restored relationship with you, you better believe he will forgive any trespass that seems to stand in your way now.

God doesn't operate the way the world does. He doesn't make you pay the penalty for your own sin. Instead, he offers perfect grace. In story after story in Scripture God turns the systems of the world on their head through the concept of grace. In the story of the prodigal son, the father allowed the son to dishonor him, set aside his rightful punishment, and threw a huge party for his wayward child returned home. He didn't wait. He didn't make him work for his redemption. He immediately offered him forgiveness freely in grace. God offers you the same today. Don't attempt to pay for your own sin by separating yourself from the fullness of relationship with God. Jesus paid the only price necessary by his own death. Live in light of God's grace. Offer your heart to God freely. Let him work out redemption in every area of your life that you might more fully experience the wonderful relationship you have available to you with God.

GUIDED PRAYER

1. Take time to reflect on the amazing grace of God.

"He sent redemption to his people; he has commanded his covenant forever. Holy and awesome is his name!" Psalm 111:9

2. Talk to God about any area of your life you feel separated from him through sin or a lack of understanding. Where in your life do you not feel grace? What part of your thinking is dominated by condemnation or negativity?

3. Ask God for forgiveness and understanding of his grace in those areas of your life. Receive the freedom that comes from his presence and forgiveness.

God works tirelessly to lead you into the fullness of relationship with him because he loves you. You are his child. He knows everything about you; he's created you, and he loves spending time with you. May your affections be stirred towards him today. May you know and experience his love in mighty and transformative ways. May you spend your day in God's presence, changed and empowered by the reality of his boundless grace.

Extended Reading: Ephesians 1

The Wisdom of God

DAY 11

DEVOTIONAL

Your heavenly Father is perfectly wise. Everything he does is perfect. Every thought and idea he has is filled with complete wisdom. What's more, through the Holy Spirit you have access to that wisdom. James 1:5 says, *"If any of you lacks wisdom, let him ask God, who gives generously to all without reproach, and it will be given him."* Your God loves you so much that he's just waiting to bestow on you his vast wisdom. He never wants you to suffer from a lack of knowledge. So often, we are taught that God only reveals to us what we absolutely have to know right before we need to know it. But that's not the truth of Scripture. James 1:5 proves that. Your God gives his wisdom *"generously!"*

Not only is the wisdom of God given to you generously if you ask, but it also has with it incredible attributes. James 3:17 says, *"The wisdom from above is first pure, then peaceable, gentle, open to reason, full of mercy and good fruits, impartial and sincere."* The wisdom of God will do incredible things for your life. With it comes the very nature of God. James 3:17 could just as easily have said that God is *"pure, then peaceable, gentle, open to reason, full of mercy and good fruits, impartial and sincere."* So when you receive the wisdom God bestows upon you, you are receiving many of the attributes of God himself.

> *"If any of you lacks wisdom, let him ask God, who gives generously to all without reproach, and it will be given him."*

JAMES 1:5

The wisdom of God is unlike any other way of thinking you'll find. 1 Corinthians 3:18-20 says, *"Let no one deceive himself. If anyone among you thinks that he is wise in this age, let him become a fool that he may become wise. For the wisdom of this world is folly with God. For it is written, 'He catches the wise in their craftiness,' and again, 'The Lord knows the thoughts of the wise, that they are futile.'"* Jesus taught us in Matthew 10:39, *"Whoever finds his life will lose it, and whoever loses his life for my sake will find it."* The path he is guiding you to is the way out of the stress that worldly ambition and success will assuredly cause. He's guiding you to a life of abundant peace. When you forgo the wisdom of this world for his, you will undoubtedly appear more foolish to some. But you will have found a way of living free from the burdens of the world. God's wisdom leads you to a life truly hidden with Christ, lost in the sea of his love and mercy.

Ask God for his wisdom today. Read his word with the guidance of the Spirit. God is waiting patiently to reveal everything you have the desire to seek out. Proverbs 25:2 says, *"It is the glory of God to conceal things, but the glory of kings is to search things out."* Ask him for his wisdom today, and live the abundant life God has planned for you.

GUIDED PRAYER

1. Meditate on the amazing qualities of the God's wisdom. Let meditation stir up within you a desire to think like God.

"But the wisdom from above is first pure, then peaceable, gentle, open to reason, full of mercy and good fruits, impartial and sincere." James 3:17

2. Where in your life do you need God's wisdom?
Maybe you need to know how to see yourself. Maybe you have a situation in which you could really use some guidance. Think about the areas in your life in which you need God's help.

3. Ask God for his wisdom. Have faith in response to his word that he gives wisdom generously, and receive and implement anything he shows you.

"If any of you lacks wisdom, let him ask God, who gives generously to all without reproach, and it will be given him." James 1:5

The wisdom of God won't do much for you if you don't choose to implement God's thinking over the world's. If you continuously work for the favor of man and worldly success in light of what you know to be God's truth, you will continue to experience the consequences of a life lived foolishly. God's word must be implemented to produce fruit. You have to choose to live in light of your position in Christ for transcendent peace to become the norm in your life. God gives wisdom to you freely when you ask. The question before you today is simply whether or not you will choose to trust God and implement it.

Extended Reading: 1 Corinthians 3

No Better Friend

DAY 12

DEVOTIONAL

Revelation 3:20 reveals amazing insight into the relationship God desires with us, his crown of creation. In it Jesus says, *"Behold, I stand at the door and knock. If anyone hears my voice and opens the door, I will come in to him and eat with him, and he with me."* Do you know that God wants to be friends with you? Just as a friend would ask you out to a meal, God longs to spend time with you. Every day God is knocking on the door of your heart. If you are willing to open your heart to him and listen, you can spend time with God in ways more boundless and satisfying than you could with any other friend.

"Behold, I stand at the door and knock. If anyone hears my voice and opens the door, I will come in to him and eat with him, and he with me."

REVELATION 3:20

Where in your life do you need God's friendship today? John 15:15 says, *"No longer do I call you servants, for the servant does not know what his master is doing; but I have called you friends, for all that I have heard from my Father I have made known to you."* The story of the gospel is God losing relationship with the crown of his creation, you and me, and through the death of Jesus gaining restored relationship with us. He has been working tirelessly from the very first sin just to be able to call you and me friends again. What you desire from friends around you is completely available to you in God and to even greater depths!

If you need a friend to talk to, God is standing at the door of your heart asking to come in and listen— *"Behold, I stand at the door and knock."* If you need advice, the Holy Spirit who authored Scripture is waiting to reveal to you the wisdom of God—*"When the Spirit of truth comes, he will guide you into all the truth, for he will not speak on his own authority, but whatever he hears he will speak, and he will declare to you the things that are to come"* (John 16:13). If you need to laugh, God longs to bring you unfathomable joy—*"When the Lord restored the fortunes of Zion, we were like those who dream. Then our mouth was filled with laughter, and our tongue with shouts of joy then they said among the nations, 'The Lord has done great things for them.' The Lord has done great things for us; we are glad"* (Psalm 126:1-3).

You have a best friend in God. He is not distant. What was true for the psalmist in Psalm 73:23-26 is true for us, *"I am continually with you; you hold my right hand. You guide me with your counsel, and afterward you will receive me to glory. Whom have I in heaven but you? And there is nothing on earth that I desire besides you. My flesh and my heart may fail, but God is the strength of my heart and my portion forever."*

Spend time in God's presence today. Listen to him knocking on the door of your heart and invite him to come in and meet with you. Let his friendship heal the broken places of your heart that need his love. He offers himself freely to you today. He's gone to unimaginable lengths to be able to simply spend time with you. Lay the table of your heart bare before him, and let his smile restore to you the joy of your salvation.

GUIDED PRAYER

1. Spend some time meditating on God's desire for friendship with you.

"No longer do I call you servants, for the servant does not know what his master is doing; but I have called you friends, for all that I have heard from my Father I have made known to you."
John 15:15

2. Open your heart to God and receive his presence.
Receive the peace and joy that comes from being in the presence of your heavenly Father.

"Behold, I stand at the door and knock. If anyone hears my voice and opens the door, I will come in to him and eat with him, and he with me." Revelation 3:20

3. Spend time simply enjoying your friendship with God.
Talk to him about anything you desire. Receive his joy over you.

"I am continually with you; you hold my right hand. You guide me with your counsel, and afterward you will receive me to glory. Whom have I in heaven but you? And there is nothing on earth that I desire besides you. My flesh and my heart may fail, but God is the strength of my heart and my portion forever."
Psalm 73:23-26

Friendships aren't built in a day, but over lifetimes. You have all of eternity to spend getting to know God. After spending consistent time with him, he truly will become your best friend. He will be the person you run to when you have a problem. He will be the source of your joy, peace, and life. Every day, you have the choice to do life with God or on your own. And you have an enemy working to lead you to choose the latter. The more consistently you spend time with God, the easier that decision will become. Once you know the goodness and reality of God there is no going back. Enjoy God today. Walk in the abundant life of restored relationship with him. Answer his call whenever he knocks on the door of your heart. There is no better way you could choose to spend your days and no better friend than God.

Extended Reading: John 15

Being the Child of God

DEVOTIONAL

You are the child of God, brought into his family by the power and grace of Jesus' sacrifice for you. As believers, we hear we are God's children. But often we don't live our lives in response to that truth and instead live out of the mindset of an orphan. Children don't worry when they have a good father. They don't wonder if they'll be able to eat, if they're loved or if they have a place in this world. The unconditional love of a parent lays a foundation for them to have secure peace and joy. Your God desires the same for you. God wants to lay an unshakable foundation for you based solely on his love for you as his child so that when the storms come and waves crash over you, you remain strong in your identity.

"And because you are sons, God has sent the Spirit of his Son into our hearts, crying, 'Abba! Father!' So you are no longer a slave, but a son, and if a son, then an heir through God."

GALATIANS 4:6-7

First, let's look at what Scripture says about you, and then take some time to respond to God's word in faith. John 1:12-13 says, *"But to all who did receive him, who believed in his name, he gave the right to become children of God, who were born, not of blood nor of the will of the flesh nor of the will of man, but of God."* Galatians 4:6-7 says, *"And because you are sons, God has sent the Spirit of his Son into our hearts, crying, 'Abba! Father!' So you are no longer a slave, but a son, and if a son, then an heir through God."* Finally, 2 Corinthians 6:18 says, *"And I will be a father to you, and you shall be sons and daughters to me, says the Lord Almighty."* Through adoption into God's family you are now a co-heir with Christ. Romans 8:17 says that we are God's children, *"and if children, then heirs—heirs of God and fellow heirs with Christ."* You were born again into God's family when you asked Jesus to be your Lord and Savior.

So what does it mean to be God's child? What does it mean to be a co-heir with Christ? It means that all that is God's is yours. He shares with you his kingdom. You have a Father who gives you amazing gifts. You have a Father who absolutely loves spending time with you. Your heavenly Dad's love for you knows no bounds. His love is pervasive, powerful, and freely given. You no longer need to worry about whether you have a place in this world. There's no need to concern yourself with whether you will have clothes or food. You no longer have to live in pursuit of the opinions of those around you. God enjoys you. He has a plan for you. He doesn't take being your Father lightly. He takes complete ownership of his responsibility. He will strengthen you, teach you, develop you, and give you a life of passion and meaning. To be the child of God is to be loved, liked, and completely cared for.

So how can you live in response to God's word? How can you get out of the mindset of an orphan? You must have faith that God is who he says he is and believe he will do what he's promised to do. Romans 10:17 says that *"faith comes from hearing, and hearing through the word of Christ."* You have heard the word of the Lord today. You are his child. He promises to provide for you. So have faith! Faith isn't something you just conjure up. It's a response to God's faithfulness. God has and will be faithful to you. Allow his word to stir up faith within you today. Live in response to his promises and allow the peace and joy of being God's child to lay an unshakable foundation for you today.

67

GUIDED PRAYER

1. Meditate on the truth of God's word. You are his child. Let it sink deep into your heart.

"And because you are sons, God has sent the Spirit of his Son into our hearts, crying, 'Abba! Father!' So you are no longer a slave, but a son, and if a son, then an heir through God." Galatians 4:6-7

2. Now ask the Spirit to show you any mindsets you have that don't line up with his word. Where in your life do you feel stressed? What makes you feel like you don't have what it takes? Where do you feel unloved or unliked?

3. Now ask God to speak to those places. What does it mean for you to be his child? What about your life should be different? Cast off those mindsets and realign your way of thinking with God's.

"And I will be a father to you, and you shall be sons and daughters to me, says the Lord Almighty." 2 Corinthians 6:18

God's love for you is sure. There is nothing you could ever do to remove yourself from his family. Once you are his child, you are his forever. As a Christian you are living under God's grace, not works. God loves you because he loves you—not because of what you think about yourself or what you do. Therefore, release any thoughts you have of yourself that don't line up with God's word. Let go of any burdens you're carrying today in light of his love. And experience the transforming power of a life lived in response to the faithfulness of God.

Extended Reading: Galatians 4

The Faithfulness of God

DEVOTIONAL

Numbers 23:19 describes a foundational aspect of God's character, his faithfulness. Scripture says, *"God is not man, that he should lie, or a son of man, that he should change his mind. Has he said, and will he not do it? Or has he spoken, and will he not fulfill it?"* As believers, we need a revelation of God's faithfulness. Being able to fully trust God is the beginning of living an abundant life. If you don't fully believe

"God is not man, that he should lie, or a son of man, that he should change his mind. Has he said, and will he not do it? Or has he spoken, and will he not fulfill it?"

NUMBERS 23:19

that God is faithful to lead you into the best possible life you could live, then you won't seek out his will, trust him with your possessions, or be able to fully enjoy his presence.

God's word promises us in Numbers 23:19 that God is perfectly faithful, steadfast, and true. Philippians 1:6 says, *"And I am sure of this, that he who began a good work in you will bring it to completion at the day of Jesus Christ."* Romans 8:28 promises, *"We know that for those who love God all things work together for good, for those who are called according to his purpose."* Your God is wholly faithful to you. No matter what you do, he will be there for you. His faithfulness isn't dependent upon your works. All he requires is a willing heart to bring about the incredible fruit of the Spirit in your life.

You aren't meant to live life apart from the knowledge of God's faithfulness. You aren't meant to live with the weight of doing life on your own. Man may fail you, but your God will not. Family and friends may not be there when you need them, but your God will always be there for you.

Where do you feel on your own? In what ways do you need a fresh revelation of God's faithfulness? He promises to be true to you. He promises to see you through any situation you find yourself in. Isaiah 54:10 says, *"'For the mountains may depart and the hills be removed, but my steadfast love shall not depart from you, and my covenant of peace shall not be removed,' says the Lord, who has compassion on you."* Faithfulness is foundational to the very character of God. God's steadfast love for you is more sure than the very ground you walk on.

So respond to God's faithfulness today. Let his promises steady the parts of your life that feel unsure. As you step outside today, take time to look at the world around you. Think about the things you've put your trust in. And remember, God promises that his faithfulness will outlast anything your eyes can see. May your affections for him be stirred today. May you respond to his faithfulness with your own. And may you experience the love and joy of a Father who loves you perfectly and completely.

GUIDED PRAYER

1. Meditate on God's promise to be faithful to you.

"God is not man, that he should lie, or a son of man, that he should change his mind. Has he said, and will he not do it? Or has he spoken, and will he not fulfill it?" Numbers 23:19

"Now may the God of peace himself sanctify you completely, and may your whole spirit and soul and body be kept blameless at the coming of our Lord Jesus Christ. He who calls you is faithful; he will surely do it." 1 Thessalonians 5:23-24

"Let us hold fast the confession of our hope without wavering, for he who promised is faithful." Hebrews 10:23

2. Now reflect on your own life. Where in your life do you feel unsure? What situations seem to toss your emotions around like a boat in the middle of a storm? Where do you need a firmer foundation today?

3. Ask the Spirit for a revelation of God's faithfulness in those areas. Ask God to help you trust in his promise of faithfulness. Ask him how he plans on bringing peace to those areas that are disturbing you today. Listen to him as he speaks.

Not only does God promise you his faithfulness, but he will actually reveal to you how he is working in your life. You can ask him for his plans, and he will show you! You can ask him how he feels about you and your life, and he will tell you! Within his promise of faithfulness is the promise of his voice. You will hear him speak today if you open your heart, listen to the Spirit and be alert for God to speak through whatever avenue he chooses. Your heavenly Father loves you. Spend your day establishing the foundation of his faithfulness in your own life. And experience a life lived in the abundance of God's assurance and peace.

Extended Reading: Isaiah 54

God's character

03

WEEK

"Jesus Christ is the same yesterday and today and forever." Hebrews 13:8

WEEKLY OVERVIEW

Too often we feel that God is distant or separated from us. Too often we allow misconceptions or lies to place a rift between us and experiencing God. It's in reminding ourselves of God's character that lies are broken and a pathway is laid for us to encounter his tangible love. Open your heart and mind and receive fresh revelation of the goodness of God this week. Allow your affections to be stirred and your heart to be filled with desire to seek the face of your heavenly Father.

Sanctification in the Waiting

DEVOTIONAL

1 Corinthians 13:4 tells us, *"Love is patient."* Patience is a part of love that doesn't feel fun at the beginning. It feels like an act of self-control rather than passion, as if the two aren't perfectly connected. And it often comes across as a sign of weakness rather than an attribute of the bold and powerful we so often admire. But Scripture teaches us a different view of patience. 2 Peter 3:8-9 says, *"But do not overlook this one fact, beloved, that with the Lord one day is as a thousand years, and a thousand years as one day. The Lord is not slow to fulfill his promise as some count slowness,* *but is patient toward you, not wishing that any should perish, but that all should reach repentance."* God, in his passionate desire for restored relationship with all his children, has perfect patience toward us. His passion leads him to patience. And it is in his desire to see us grow in all manner of holiness and godliness that he waits to bring about the restoration of all things to him with the coming of the new heavens and earth. Let's open our hearts today to become more like our heavenly Father and allow him to create in us a heart worthy of him who has so patiently loved us.

> *"For God is working in you, giving you the*
> *desire and the power to do what pleases him."*

PHILIPPIANS 2:13 (NLT)

I fear that much of the bride of Christ is living day-to-day, getting by until Jesus returns. And I fear that in our complacency we are not engaging in the purposes for which Christ came. God's intention here is to use us to bring about a saving knowledge to all those around us. His plan was for restoration of relationship here, not just biding our time while suffering from a lack of his reality working in our lives. 2 Peter 3:14 says, *"Therefore, beloved, since you are waiting for [new heavens and a new earth], be diligent to be found by him without spot or blemish, and at peace."* And Hebrews 12:3-11 says,

It is for discipline that you have to endure. God is treating you as sons. For what son is there whom his father does not discipline? If you are left without discipline, in which all have participated, then you are illegitimate children and not sons. Besides this, we have had earthly fathers who disciplined us and we respected them. Shall we not much more be subject to the Father of spirits and live? For they disciplined us for a short time as it seemed best to them, but he disciplines us for our good, that we may share his holiness. For the moment all discipline seems painful rather than pleasant, but later it yields the peaceful fruit of righteousness to those who have been trained by it.

Because God loves us he does not desire for us to remain as we were or as we are. His plan is to do such a work in us that we live on this earth as Jesus did. But he is entirely patient to accomplish this work. He is entirely patient with our sanctification.

When I began engaging in the process of sanctification I was filled with frustration. For the first time I began to see all the dirt and muck covering up this beautiful gift of a new nature God had given me. I felt like I was never going to be able to get through all the sin that seemed to so entangle me to my old nature, and I was right. Scripture teaches us that it is God, in his patience, who produces holiness and godliness. In my own strength I have no ability to change my heart. My only job is to engage with him and allow him to work in and through me. Philippians 2:13 says, *"For it is God who works in you, both to will and to work for his good pleasure."* The NLT version says it this way: *"For God is working in you, giving you the desire and the power to do what pleases him."* God's desire isn't for us to engage in works that have the appearance of morality but aren't flowing from the true desire of our hearts. His longing is to mold and shape our hearts by his love into a perfect reflection of his heart so that we might live true lives of holiness out of the overflow of what he has done in us. Only he can accomplish such a work. Only he can fill us with the ability to truly love. And as 2 Peter 3:9 tells us, he is patient to do so.

Spend time in prayer discovering the patient heart of your heavenly Father. Spend time allowing his love to draw you into the process of sanctification. And allow the Holy Spirit to do a mighty work in you today, bringing about holiness and godliness where it seemed only sin and worldliness could dwell.

GUIDED PRAYER

1. Meditate on the patient heart of your heavenly Father. Reflect on how his patience comes from his passionate love for us.

"The Lord is not slow to fulfill his promise as some count slowness, but is patient toward you, not wishing that any should perish, but that all should reach repentance." 2 Peter 3:9

"The Lord is merciful and gracious, slow to anger and abounding in steadfast love." Psalm 103:8

2. Now meditate on God's desire to produce holiness and godliness in you. Allow this truth to grow in connection to God's love. His love leads him to discipline and work in us.

"Since all these things are thus to be dissolved, what sort of people ought you to be in lives of holiness and godliness, waiting for and hastening the coming of the day of God, because of which the heavens will be set on fire and dissolved, and the heavenly bodies will melt as they burn!" 2 Peter 3:11

"It is for discipline that you have to endure. God is treating you as sons. For what son is there whom his father does not discipline? If you are left without discipline, in which all have participated, then you are illegitimate children and not sons. Besides this, we have had earthly fathers who disciplined us and we respected them. Shall we not much more be subject to the Father of spirits and live? For they disciplined us for a short time as it seemed best to them, but he disciplines us for our good, that we may share his holiness. For the moment all discipline seems painful rather than pleasant, but later it yields the peaceful fruit of righteousness to those who have been trained by it." Hebrews 12:3-11

3. Now engage in the process of sanctification with the Holy Spirit. Allow him to reveal to you places in your life that do not align with your new nature. Ask him to take you to the source of your sin and correct your understanding so that you might walk in holiness today. Allow your desire to live like Jesus be stirred up in his presence. Do not work in your own strength but with the power and love of the Spirit who dwells within you.

"For God is working in you, giving you the desire and the power to do what pleases him." Philippians 2:13 (NLT)

"We know that our old self was crucified with him in order that the body of sin might be brought to nothing, so that we would no longer be enslaved to sin." Romans 6:6

"May grace and peace be multiplied to you in the knowledge of God and of Jesus our Lord. His divine power has granted to us all things that pertain to life and godliness, through the knowledge of him who called us to his own glory and excellence, by which he has granted to us his precious and very great promises, so that through them you may become partakers of the divine nature, having escaped from the corruption that is in the world because of sinful desire." 2 Peter 1:2-4

God has promised to deliver us from this world. We have hope that the trials and tribulations of this world will not be forever. Jesus is coming again to restore all things to be as they should. Find peace and joy in the fact that God is both working now and will work then. He is both healing, transforming, and freeing us now as he will then. In his patience he is passionately waiting for more to come to know him. May your life be a reflection of his perfect love to all those around you, that Jesus might gain the due reward of his suffering through you.

Extended Reading: Romans 6

God Our Great Protector

DEVOTIONAL

I used to be scared to death any time I heard someone talking about the devil. He always seemed so cunning, too cunning, for me to handle. I saw Christian after Christian enveloped in temptation fall away from what seemed to be God's will for their life. I heard about the ways in which the world was so tricked by his schemes. And I thought I would never be able to fully defeat this strong and cunning foe.

Do you feel that way? Does your enemy seem too strong to defeat? Does he seem too cunning to outwit? Does it feel like he has so grasped you in his clutches that escape is impossible? The most important fact for you to know about Satan is that he is the father of all lies. John 8:44 says, *"He was a murderer from the beginning, and does not stand in the truth, because there is no truth in him. When he lies,* *he speaks out of his own character, for he is a liar and the father of lies."* Let that truth sink in for a minute. Everything the devil tells you is a lie. He cannot speak full truth. Everything he tells you is in opposition to God, who is the author of all truth. All of the devil's whispers about his strength and your inability to defeat him are in opposition to the word of God. May we find blissful freedom today in the powerful words of our loving, truthful heavenly Father. May we allow his Spirit to come in and correct the lies of the enemy we have believed so that we might walk in the abundant life available to us through Christ.

2 Thessalonians 3:3 says, *"But the Lord is faithful. He will establish you and guard you against the evil one."* Our heavenly Father is a perfect, capable protector from Satan. He promises to establish us

"But the Lord is faithful. He will establish
you and guard you against the evil one."

2 THESSALONIANS 3:3

and guard us. He is always with us and always knows exactly what we need in order to withstand the temptations of the evil one. 1 Corinthians 10:13 teaches us, *"No temptation has overtaken you that is not common to man. God is faithful, and he will not let you be tempted beyond your ability, but with the temptation he will also provide the way of escape, that you may be able to endure it."* The Holy Spirit will always provide us an exit from temptation. Always. There will never be a temptation that comes your way that you cannot escape when you are under the leadership of the Holy Spirit.

One of the enemy's most used weapons is the lie that you cannot defeat him. He reminds us of our past failures, of his great cunning ways, and of his victories over us. He whispers that he is stronger than us and that we will give in eventually. All lies. Past failures do not have to dictate the outcome of future battles. In fact, if we will allow the Holy Spirit to use past failures to reveal to us ways in which he longed to lead us away from temptation, past sins become stepping stones on which we achieve future victories. Titus 2:11-14 says, *"For the grace of God has appeared, bringing salvation for all people, training us to renounce ungodliness and worldly passions, and to live self-controlled, upright, and godly lives in the present age, waiting for our blessed hope, the appearing of the glory of our great God and Savior Jesus Christ, who gave himself for us to redeem us*

from all lawlessness and to purify for himself a people for his own possession who are zealous for good works." God's grace lays the foundation for our victory over the enemy, not our own works. It was in his grace that Jesus died to set us free from this world and restore us to God. His grace leads us away from temptation. And it's his grace that he offers us every time we confess our sins to him. God's grace is powerful, freeing, perfect, and full of love. He knows our weaknesses. He knows our frame. But he is also perfectly capable of being strong in our weakness if we allow him to be.

You never have to fall into temptation again. God has a perfect plan for every temptation that comes your way. The enemy is not stronger than you. He is not more cunning than you. And he will not have victory over you because you have God, and God has defeated him. Your protector and guard is the very God who defeated the enemy at the cross and will throw him into the lake of fire, resulting in his ultimate destruction. That God lives inside of you, has grace for you, and plans to use your past failures and current weaknesses to powerfully defeat your enemy.

Spend time in prayer meditating on the truth of God's power over the enemy. Reflect on your own life and allow the Spirit to take your past failures and turn them into future victories. And allow Scripture to fill you with truth to combat the future lies of the enemy.

85

GUIDED PRAYER

1. Meditate on God's faithful protection over you.

"But the Lord is faithful. He will establish you and guard you against the evil one." 2 Thessalonians 3:3

"No temptation has overtaken you that is not common to man. God is faithful, and he will not let you be tempted beyond your ability, but with the temptation he will also provide the way of escape, that you may be able to endure it." 1 Corinthians 10:13

2. Reflect on your past failures. Ask the Holy Spirit to reveal to you ways in which he was leading you away from temptation. What did he desire you to do so that you might walk in victory over your enemy? In what ways did he desire to protect you?

3. Allow the Spirit to empower you for future victories. Ask him to make you more aware of his leadership in future temptations and to empower you to follow him. Meditate on the truth of who you are in Christ and the truth of the enemy's plans for you. May Scripture and the Holy Spirit empower you during this time for every temptation the enemy has planned for you.

"For the grace of God has appeared, bringing salvation for all people, training us to renounce ungodliness and worldly passions, and to live self-controlled, upright, and godly lives in the present age, waiting for our blessed hope, the appearing of the glory of our great God and Savior Jesus Christ, who gave himself for us to redeem us from all lawlessness and to purify for himself a people for his own possession who are zealous for good works." Titus 2:11-14

"There is therefore now no condemnation for those who are in Christ Jesus." Romans 8:1

"What shall we say then? Are we to continue in sin that grace may abound? By no means! How can we who died to sin still live in it? Do you not know that all of us who have been baptized into Christ Jesus were baptized into his death? We were buried therefore with him by baptism into death, in order that, just as Christ was raised from the dead by the glory of the Father, we too might walk in newness of life. For if we have been united with him in a death like his, we shall certainly be united with him in a resurrection like his." Romans 6:1-5

"Submit yourselves therefore to God. Resist the devil, and he will flee from you." James 4:7

"The thief comes only to steal and kill and destroy. I came that they may have life and have it abundantly." John 10:10

It's critical that we renew our mind to the truth of who we are in Christ on a daily basis. The enemy will never stop tempting us because he will never stop hating us and the God whom we belong to. But you can achieve victory over the enemy every single time because victory is already yours in Christ. You are the enemy's no longer. You have been given a new nature of righteousness. The most powerful weapon you have is God's word. Memorize Scripture about your new nature and allow it to redefine the way you see yourself. Walk in light of the incredible grace of God working in and through your life today.

Extended Reading: 1 Corinthians 10

87

God is Trustworthy

DEVOTIONAL

Our heavenly Father calls us, his children, to place our trust solely in him for provision, well-being, and guidance. We see God call his people to a lifestyle of trust throughout Scripture, but time and time again the people of God take matters into their own hands. Why is trust so difficult? Why do we have a hard time placing the burden of provision, well-being, and guidance in the capable hands of our heavenly Father? The only good posture of our hearts is total trust in our God. The only way we will experience the full reality, love, and power of our heavenly Father is in trusting him. It's when we trust him that we allow him to move in our lives. It's when we trust him that we position ourselves to receive the powerful working of the Holy Spirit. It's when we trust him that we allow him to work in and through us to see his will done on the earth. So, let's allow God's word to be our guide today as we open our hearts to receiving the courage and faith to place our trust in God.

Psalm 9:10 speaks to the core of trusting in God: *"And those who know your name put their trust in you, for you, O Lord, have not forsaken those who seek you."* Trusting God is first and foremost a matter of knowing his character and faithfulness. We must know his name, or who he is, and know in our heart of hearts that he will not forsake us. Trusting God starts with a knowledge of his trustworthiness, but must make its way down to the heart. If we don't allow God's character and faithfulness to become a transformative reality of our heart, we will never bear the fruit of trust. So in order to begin a lifestyle of trust in areas in which we have taken control for ourselves, we must begin by asking God for a fresh revelation of his character and faithfulness. We must see God for who he is, reflect on his faithfulness as demonstrated in Scripture, in the lives of other believers, and in our own lives, and allow these revelations to transform our hearts' desires and bear the fruit of trust.

Oftentimes it takes me being at my wit's end, where there is nothing possible left for me to do, before I pray and ask God for his help. In reality, I should begin every part of my life with surrender to the Holy Spirit's power and guidance. I should follow God's leadership from the beginning. Isaiah 26:3-4 says, *"You keep him in perfect peace whose mind is stayed on you, because he trusts in you. Trust in the Lord forever, for the Lord God*

> *"And those who know your name put their trust in you, for you, O Lord, have not forsaken those who seek you."*
>
> **PSALM 9:10**

is an everlasting rock." My life should be a continual response to the love and faithfulness of God rather than a trial of my own strength ending in cries of desperation to my heavenly Father who longed to help me all along. God's desire is that we would be a people marked by the peace that only comes from continual trust in response to his trustworthiness. Continual peace comes from continual trust.

Psalm 37:3-5 offers what I believe to be a blueprint for the abundant life God desires for each of us. David writes, *"Trust in the Lord, and do good; dwell in the land and befriend faithfulness. Delight yourself in the Lord, and he will give you the desires of your heart. Commit your way to the Lord; trust in him, and he will act."* When we place our trust solely in God we are filled with delight in him in place of the burden and weight of living life in our own strength. And when we delight ourselves fully in God, our desires come into line with his, allowing us to simply *"do good"* and *"dwell in the land."* If we will trust in God he will both fill us with the desires he has for us and then satisfy those desires. When the people of God respond to his faithfulness with trust, he does

mighty and incredible works. God delivered the entire nation of Israel through the trust of one man, Moses. He destroyed the walls of Jericho through the faithful marching of his people. He scattered the Midianites in response to the trust of Gideon. He delivered Paul and Silas from prison as they worshipped him in trust. The stories go on and on, but they all have this in common: God spoke his desires to his people, his people trusted him at his word in response to his character and faithfulness, and he did a mighty work in their favor.

Where do you need a powerful work of your heavenly Father today? Where do you need his help and guidance? Spend time meditating on the character and past faithfulness of your heavenly Father and place your trust in him in response to his trustworthiness. Your God loves you and longs to help you. He has a plan to deliver you from whatever comes against you. Just as he destroyed the enemies of his people time and time again, he will help you overcome whatever obstacle stands in your way today. Place your hope and trust in God and follow him as he leads you to a life of victory and freedom.

GUIDED PRAYER

1. Meditate on the character and faithful works of God.

"God is not man, that he should lie, or a son of man, that he should change his mind. Has he said, and will he not do it? Or has he spoken, and will he not fulfill it?" Numbers 23:19

"The Lord is good, a stronghold in the day of trouble; he knows those who take refuge in him." Nahum 1:7

"Jesus Christ is the same yesterday and today and forever." Hebrews 13:8

2. Reflect on your own life. Where do you need God's help today? Where do you need his favor or guidance? Where do you need a miracle?

3. Place your trust in God, ask for his help, and follow his leadership. Spend time placing your trust solely in him. If it feels too difficult to trust him completely, ask for his help! Ask him to uncover whatever lie is keeping you from trusting him. Ask him to reveal his nearness, love, and power to you. Trust is meant to be a response, not something you conjure up. Allow him to reveal himself in deeper ways so that you can simply respond to his overwhelming reality, love, power, and faithfulness.

"And those who know your name put their trust in you, for you, O Lord, have not forsaken those who seek you." Psalm 9:10

"Trust in him at all times, O people; pour out your heart before him; God is a refuge for us." Psalm 62:8

"Trust in the Lord, and do good; dwell in the land and befriend faithfulness. Delight yourself in the Lord, and he will give you the desires of your heart. Commit your way to the Lord; trust in him, and he will act." Psalm 37:3-5

May you grow in your knowledge of the trustworthiness of your God today. May you experience the joy of having the Creator of all working in the details of your own life. God is not too busy for you today. He doesn't have better or bigger things planned than your problems. He is infinite, vast, all-powerful, all-knowing, and all-loving. He longs to work in the little things along with the big things. Listen to him as he speaks Isaiah 43:1-2 over you today:

Fear not, for I have redeemed you; I have called you by name, you are mine. When you pass through the waters, I will be with you; and through the rivers, they shall not overwhelm you; when you walk through fire you shall not be burned, and the flame shall not consume you.

Extended Reading: Psalm 37

God is Worthy of Devotion

DAY 18

DEVOTIONAL

Throughout Scripture we see a powerful principle exemplified: when God is seen for who he truly is, the natural response of the seer is full and absolute devotion. When God reveals his glory, love, power, holiness, and splendor, the seer responds with absolute commitment and worship. I believe that God would reveal himself to us today in simple but mighty ways. I

"Holy, holy, holy is the Lord of hosts;
the whole earth is full of his glory!"

ISAIAH 6:3

believe that he longs for us to see him as he truly is, and that his chief desire is our devotion. May we see God face-to-face today and be forever changed by a fresh revelation of this God who would give up everything for relationship with us.

Isaiah 6 exemplifies both a vision of God and a response of devotion. Isaiah has an open vision of the majesty of God in heaven. He sees God on his throne and hears angels declaring his holiness and splendor by saying, *"Holy, holy, holy is the Lord of hosts; the whole earth is full of his glory!"* (Isaiah 6:3). And in response to this vision Isaiah 6:8 says, *"And I heard the voice of the Lord saying, 'Whom shall I send, and who will go for us?' Then I said, 'Here I am! Send me.'"* Isaiah responds to seeing God with full devotion.

God doesn't ask for your devotion the way man does. He doesn't offer you ultimatums or transactionally based benefits if you will love him. Devotion to him is meant to be the natural response of seeing God for who he is, because he is inherently worthy of every bit of devotion we can bring to him. He is worthy of our allegiance because he is the King of Kings. He is worthy of our obedience because his

will is both knowable and perfect. He is worthy of our worship because he is the almighty God to whom all creation offers ceaseless praise. And he is worthy of our heart because he is the God of love and mercy who has created us for relationship with him.

Too often we mistake God's mercy and grace as opportunities to go our own way and come back to him as we please or when we need something. Too often we treat his love as an opiate for our problems rather than the foundation on which we devote our lives in humble submission to him. God is patient. He is kind. He will never force or manipulate us into loving him. But his patience, kindness, and gentleness do not change the fact that he is King of kings, Lord of lords, and Creator of all, and that he is worthy and deserving of our ceaseless devotion.

Run to meet your God in the secret place today. Look upon his face and see him for both the loving and majestic God he is. He longs to reveal his nature to you. He longs for you to search out the depths of him and be awed by his wonder and mystery. Spend time in prayer meeting with your loving heavenly Father and responding to his nature with your love, worship, and devotion.

93

GUIDED PRAYER

1. Meditate on the majesty, holiness, and love of God. Allow Scripture and the Holy Spirit to guide you into a direct encounter with the living God. Ask God to reveal his nearness, holiness and love to you in a fresh way.

"In the year that King Uzziah died I saw the Lord sitting upon a throne, high and lifted up; and the train of his robe filled the temple. Above him stood the seraphim. Each had six wings: with two he covered his face, and with two he covered his feet, and with two he flew. And one called to another and said:

*'Holy, holy, holy is the Lord of hosts;
the whole earth is full of his glory!'*

And the foundations of the thresholds shook at the voice of him who called, and the house was filled with smoke. And I said: 'Woe is me! For I am lost; for I am a man of unclean lips, and I dwell in the midst of a people of unclean lips; for my eyes have seen the King, the Lord of hosts!'

Then one of the seraphim flew to me, having in his hand a burning coal that he had taken with tongs from the altar. And he touched my mouth and said: 'Behold, this has touched your lips; your guilt is taken away, and your sin atoned for.'" Isaiah 6:1-7

"I am the first and I am the last; apart from me there is no God." Isaiah 44:6

2. Spend time giving him thanks for who he is. Worship him through thanksgiving.

"Oh give thanks to the Lord, for he is good, for his steadfast love endures forever!" Psalm 107:1

"Through [Jesus] then let us continually offer up a sacrifice of praise to God, that is, the fruit of lips that acknowledge his name." Hebrews 13:15

"It is good to give thanks to the Lord, to sing praises to your name, O Most High; to declare your steadfast love in the morning, and your faithfulness by night, to the music of the lute and the harp, to the melody of the lyre. For you, O Lord, have made me glad by your work; at the works of your hands I sing for joy. How great are your works, O Lord! Your thoughts are very deep!" Psalm 92:1-5

3. Now offer God your total devotion in response to who he is. Commit to following his leadership and living your life in total obedience to him through the help of the Holy Spirit.

"Indeed, I count everything as loss because of the surpassing worth of knowing Christ Jesus my Lord." Philippians 3:8

"Love the Lord your God with all your heart and with all your soul and with all your strength." Deuteronomy 6:5

May your life be an example of a believer in love with God. May you offer God all the love, obedience, and devotion you can. All God desires is your heart. He longs to have all of you. He is completely relationship focused and completely lovesick for you. 2 Chronicles 16:9 says, "For the eyes of the Lord range throughout the earth to strengthen those whose hearts are fully committed to him." God will help you live your life in commitment to him if you allow him to. Receive the strength of the Lord and respond to his love with your devotion today.

Extended Reading: Isaiah 44

God is Good

DAY 19

DEVOTIONAL

God is good. What emotion does that fact stir in you? I know for some this phrase stirs up unspeakable joy, while others of us seem to be immune to its emotion in our lives. I believe the issue for many of us is that the phrase "God is good" is so frequently said and so infrequently experienced. For many of us we are just told that God is good from a young age, but we are seldom given the chance to experience that goodness. Goodness is something meant to be experienced and then believed, not the other way around.

*"I believe that I shall look upon the goodness
of the Lord in the land of the living!"*

PSALM 27:13

David said that he would look upon the goodness of the Lord in the land of the living. He had already seen God's goodness in his life and believed that he would see it again. He knew for a fact that God was good and therefore he sought to experience that goodness. It's that same heart that the Sons of Korah had in the famous Psalm 84, singing, *"How lovely is your dwelling place, O Lord of hosts! My soul longs, yes, faints for the courts of the Lord; my heart and flesh sing for joy to the living God . . . For a day in your courts is better than a thousand elsewhere. I would rather be a doorkeeper in the house of my God than dwell in the tents of wickedness"* (Psalm 84:1-2,10). That sounds like the worship of a good God, a goodness that had been experienced.

When was the last time you experienced the goodness of God? Psalm 33:5 says, *"The earth is full of the goodness of the Lord."* God's goodness is here, just waiting to be experienced. James 1:17 says, *"Every good gift and every perfect gift is from above, coming down from the Father of lights with whom there is no variation or shadow due to change."* God is always good, and every good and perfect gift you've received is from him! He demonstrates his goodness to us in innumerable ways, all the time. How is it then that we don't recognize it? How is it that we can be surrounded by God's goodness and not experience it?

God has proven in Scripture that he works in our midst demonstrating his goodness, but we have to take time to listen and respond to these demonstrations. In Psalm 27 God says to David, *"Seek my face,"* and David responds, *"My heart says to you, your face, Lord, do I seek."* When God says *"seek"* he uses a Hebrew word that is meant for more than one person. God calls all of us, his people, to *"seek my face."* Then in response we are to say, *"Your face, Lord, do I seek."*

Take time today to respond to God's invitation of goodness. Seek to look upon his face and to experience his goodness. He has laid a banquet table before you and is simply asking you to come and dine with him.

GUIDED PRAYER

1. Take time to quiet yourself and receive God's presence. Meditate on this verse:

"You make known to me the path of life; in your presence there is fullness of joy; at your right hand are pleasures forevermore." Psalm 16:11

2. Respond to his goodness by telling the Lord:

"My heart says to you, Your face, Lord, do I seek." Psalm 27:8

3. Make David's prayer yours today:

"One thing have I asked of the Lord, that will I seek after: that I may dwell in the house of the Lord all the days of my life, to gaze upon the beauty of the Lord and to inquire in his temple." Psalm 27:4

Take time to make that prayer your own throughout your day today. Memorize it. Write it on your heart so that you can experience the goodness of God throughout your day. It only takes a minute to receive his presence and have the joy and peace that can only be found in Christ Jesus.

Extended Reading: Psalm 27

God's Great Gift of Love

DEVOTIONAL

You need to experience the love of God. The single most important part of your day is receiving the love of your heavenly Father. Without being loved by God, you can't fully love him or others. And the Bible says in 1 Corinthians 13:1, *"If I speak in the tongues of men*

"We love because he first loved us."

1 JOHN 4:19

and of angels, but have not love, I am a noisy gong or a clanging cymbal." You're called to live your life in response to God's love, because God asks that everything you do be done in love. If what you are doing isn't done in love, it is not pleasing to him, and you can't live a lifestyle of loving others without being loved by him first.

What's more, God's desire is to completely overwhelm you with his love right now. He doesn't want to love you just so you'll love him back or love those around you. Loving God and others is a natural by-product of receiving God's love. He loves you just because he loves you.

He longs for you to live a lifestyle of love because he knows that's the absolute, most fulfilling, purposeful, and peaceful way of life for you. He longs to set you free from the burdens of living for your own gain. He longs to lead you to the path of abundant life. But it all starts with simply receiving his love.

The love of God will guide you, establish you, empower you, and fully delight you. His love will free you, compel you, and sustain you. His love for you is eternal, real, and right now. All you need to do is simply open your heart to him and set aside a little time right now to receive his amazing gift of love.

God desires to be experienced. He is living and active, but so few experience the life and love he wants to bring. Today, after receiving his love, take some time to reflect on how differently you feel and act afterwards. See if you feel a stirring of desire for God and those around you. You see, God intends for us to have his love for those around us. In loving God you receive his love for others. You care about the things the people you love care about. It is the same with God. But it all starts with simply being loved by him. There's no better time than right now, wherever you are, to receive the love of your heavenly Father.

GUIDED PRAYER

1. Ask the Holy Spirit to help you encounter the love of God. Receive the peace, love, and comfort of God. Let all your cares go and take some time to just rest in his presence.

"No, in all these things we are more than conquerors through him who loved us. For I am sure that neither death nor life, nor angels nor rulers, nor things present nor things to come, nor powers, nor height nor depth, nor anything else in all creation, will be able to separate us from the love of God in Christ Jesus our Lord." Romans 8:37-39

"You will seek me and find me, when you seek me with all your heart." Jeremiah 29:13

2. Ask God to give you revelation on his heart for you and those around you.

"For God so loved the world, that he gave his only Son, that whoever believes in him should not perish but have eternal life." John 3:16

"In this the love of God was made manifest among us, that God sent his only Son into the world, so that we might live through him. In this is love, not that we have loved God but that he loved us and sent his Son to be the propitiation for our sins. Beloved, if God so loved us, we also ought to love one another. No one has ever seen God; if we love one another, God abides in us and his love is perfected in us." 1 John 4:9-12

3. Ask the Spirit to help you love the people you encounter today with God's heart for them.

"A new commandment I give to you, that you love one another: just as I have loved you, you also are to love one another." John 13:34

Know that wherever you go, God is there. You can receive his love at any time. Whenever someone harms you today, whenever you get frustrated or stressed, take a few minutes to simply be loved by your heavenly Father. May his love be the foundation for yours in all that you do today.

Extended Reading: John 17

God Desires to be Encountered

DAY 21

DEVOTIONAL

There is a misconception in Christianity that we cannot tangibly encounter our heavenly Father. Often we're taught that we are too broken, dirty, or sinful to experience God. We're told that experiencing God is only for some people, or only for some nations and cultures. Or maybe as a result of a lack of experiencing God in the past we believe that we are made without something that allows us to encounter God. Maybe we believe that encountering God is for other people, but not for us. Nothing could be further from the truth.

*"You will seek me and find me, when
you seek me with all your heart."*

JEREMIAH 29:13

We encounter God because he desires to be encountered, not because we possess some special ability. We encounter God because he longs for us to know him, not because we are more holy than someone else. You see, encountering God is entirely based on his grace and love for us.

In Jeremiah 29:13 God promises us, *"You will seek me and find me, when you seek me with all your heart."* All that is required of us to experience God is time and energy set aside to seek him. Let that truth settle into your heart for a moment. Allow your beliefs about encountering God to be renewed by his word. You can undoubtedly experience the living, active, and most high God right now because he desires for you to. He longs for you to experience him. His greatest desire is for his children to walk in the fullness of relationship available to them. He gets excited about the idea of tangibly revealing himself to you. He is filled with joy at the idea that you would experience all the love he has in his heart for you.

Romans 8:38-39 says, *"For I am sure that neither death nor life, nor angels nor rulers, nor things present nor things to come, nor powers, nor height nor depth, nor anything else in all creation, will be able to separate us from the love of God in Christ Jesus our Lord."* Jesus did what no one else could. He made a way for us to tangibly experience our heavenly Father. Nothing can separate us from the love of our heavenly Father because Jesus has restored us completely into the fold of God. The curtain of the holy of holies was torn in two. The manifest presence of God was released by the sacrifice of Jesus for all the children of God to experience.

What do you feel is in the way of you experiencing your heavenly Father today? What past experience or present thoughts are keeping you from seeking God with all your heart. May Hebrews 10:19-22 guide you into a powerful encounter with your loving heavenly Father who desires for you to experience him today:

Therefore, brothers, since we have confidence to enter the holy places by the blood of Jesus, by the new and living way that he opened for us through the curtain, that is, through his flesh, and since we have a great priest over the house of God, let us draw near with a true heart in full assurance of faith, with our hearts sprinkled clean from an evil conscience and our bodies washed with pure water.

GUIDED PRAYER

1. Meditate on God's desire for you to encounter him.

"You will seek me and find me, when you seek me with all your heart." Jeremiah 29:13

"And he made from one man every nation of mankind to live on all the face of the earth, having determined allotted periods and the boundaries of their dwelling place, that they should seek God, in the hope that they might feel their way toward him and find him. Yet he is actually not far from each one of us." Acts 17:26-27

2. Reflect on your own life.
What do you believe stands between you and experiencing your heavenly Father? What sin do you believe has separated you from him? What belief has kept you from seeking God? What lie have you believed?

3. Allow Scripture to stir your confidence to seek the face of God.
Believe Scripture over past experiences or beliefs. God desires you to seek him!

"Therefore, brothers, since we have confidence to enter the holy places by the blood of Jesus, by the new and living way that he opened for us through the curtain, that is, through his flesh, and since we have a great priest over the house of God, let us draw near with a true heart in full assurance of faith, with our hearts sprinkled clean from an evil conscience and our bodies washed with pure water." Hebrews 10:19-22

"For I am sure that neither death nor life, nor angels nor rulers, nor things present nor things to come, nor powers, nor height nor depth, nor anything else in all creation, will be able to separate us from the love of God in Christ Jesus our Lord." Romans 8:38-39

The enemy's greatest desire for those of us already saved is to keep us from walking in the fullness of what God intends for his children. Satan can't keep us from eternal life with God, but he can keep us from experiencing the abundant life available to us here. He knows God's greatest desire is for relationship with us, so he will stop at nothing to keep God from having his desires satisfied. May your life be one marked by the fullness of what's available to you in Christ. May you be a child of God who consistently and fully experiences the love of your heavenly Father.

Extended Reading: Acts 17:22-34

God
the giver

WEEK

"My God will supply every need of yours according to his riches in glory in Christ Jesus." Philippians 4:19

WEEKLY OVERVIEW

Our heavenly Father is the giver of every good gift.
His mercies are vast, powerful, and real. His love has
the ability to completely overwhelm and satisfy every
one of our needs. Everything he gives us satisfies,
transforms, and leads us to abundant life. As we spend
this week learning about God's abundant generosity,
allow your heart to overflow with praise and thanks.
Allow his loving character to draw you close and
provide life to every dry and weary place in your soul.

God the Giver of Comfort

DAY 22

DEVOTIONAL

Isaiah 66:13 says, *"As one whom his mother comforts, so I will comfort you."* Your heavenly Father is the God of comfort. When the world takes its toll on you, he longs to wrap you in his loving embrace and bring you comfort to cover all your pain. In the face of trials and tribulations, he desires to provide you comfort in the fact that he works all things for your good. And when everything seems bent against you, he longs to sing comfort over you as he fills you with the joy and foundation of his presence.

"As one whom his mother
comforts, so I will comfort you."

ISAIAH 66:13

Jeremiah 31:13-14 says, *"'Then shall the young women rejoice in the dance, and the young men and the old shall be merry. I will turn their mourning into joy; I will comfort them, and give them gladness for sorrow. I will feast the soul of the priests with abundance, and my people shall be satisfied with my goodness,' declares the Lord."* God is in the business of turning what your enemies meant for evil into the very source of your joy. He loves to transform what was once your greatest sorrow into a reason for gladness. He longs to lead you to a life of abundance and satisfaction when the world around you seems to be dry, weary, and depleted.

God is calling out to you, *"Come to me . . . and I will give you rest"* (Matthew 11:28). He is beckoning you to open your heart to him and receive the comfort only he can provide. Sometimes opening our hearts to him can be difficult. To have our wounds be truly comforted and healed requires allowing him to come and speak to the vulnerable and sore places of our hearts. We all have wounds deep down that we have worked tirelessly to keep hidden from others and even ourselves. We all have areas of our lives that seem to hurt too greatly to bring up again, even if the very act of bringing them to the surface will be our source of healing.

When God beckons you to open up the hurt places in your life to him, know that he will only ever speak love, mercy, and forgiveness. And know that after he gets done comforting you, the area that used to be a harmful wound will be a continual source of joy, gladness, and abundant life.

Open your heart to your heavenly Father today as you pray. Allow the Spirit to guide you to wounds that need to be comforted and healed. Allow him to wrap you up in his loving presence and guide you into the abundant life he intends for you.

GUIDED PRAYER

1. Meditate on God's desire and ability to comfort your every hurt. Reflect on his promise to provide you rest where you are weary.

"'I have seen his ways, but I will heal him; I will lead him and restore comfort to him and his mourners, creating the fruit of the lips. Peace, peace, to the far and to the near,' says the Lord, 'and I will heal him.'" Isaiah 57:18-19

"'Then shall the young women rejoice in the dance, and the young men and the old shall be merry. I will turn their mourning into joy; I will comfort them, and give them gladness for sorrow. I will feast the soul of the priests with abundance, and my people shall be satisfied with my goodness,' declares the Lord." Jeremiah 31:13-14

"Come to me, all who labor and are heavy laden, and I will give you rest." Matthew 11:28

2. Ask the Spirit to guide you to areas of your heart that need to be comforted and healed. What past or present afflictions have wounded you? What's at the source of your mourning, sorrow, or pain? What does God long to heal today?

3. Ask God to show you how he feels about the person, situation, or belief that wounded you. Ask him to show you where he was through it all. Remain in his presence, allowing him to speak and provide comfort and healing. Spend as long as it takes for your hurt to be comforted.

2 Corinthians 1:3-4 says, *"Blessed be the God and Father of our Lord Jesus Christ, the Father of mercies and God of all comfort, who comforts us in all our affliction, so that we may be able to comfort those who are in any affliction, with the comfort with which we ourselves are comforted by God."* As you receive healing and comfort, God will use you to provide healing and comfort to others. God loves to use those who were broken and now healed to guide others to the place of comfort. Look for those suffering from an area in which God has healed you and comfort them with the comfort you have been shown by your heavenly Father.

Extended Reading: Jeremiah 31

God Our Great Deliverer

DAY 23

DEVOTIONAL

Our God, who delivered Daniel from the clutches of ferocious lions, David from countless pursuers, Israel from the entire nation of Egypt, and Lazarus from three days of death, promises to deliver us from whatever schemes the world has set against us. 2 Samuel 22:2-4 says, *"The Lord is my rock and my fortress and my deliverer, my God, my rock, in whom I take refuge, my shield, and the horn of my salvation, my stronghold and my refuge, my savior; you save me from violence. I call upon the Lord, who is worthy to be praised, and I am saved from my enemies."*

When we call upon the Lord our God, he works in mighty, mysterious, and perfect ways. God is perfectly able to do any and every work it takes to deliver us. Whether you need deliverance from sin, affliction, lies, or sickness, God has the power and desire to deliver you. He is both mighty and loving. He is both mysterious and real. He is both servant and King. And he sees your need and longs to meet you exactly where you are.

What enemy comes against you today? What stress, circumstance, sickness, or sin seems to have entangled you? The Lord says to you, *"Because he holds fast to me in love, I will deliver him; I will protect him, because he knows my name. When he calls to me, I will answer him; I will be with him in trouble; I will rescue him and honor him. With long life I will satisfy him and show him my salvation"* (Psalm 91:14-16). Hold fast to the hand of your heavenly Father. Don't just put your head down and muscle through whatever circumstance is before you. Instead, call on your Great Deliverer, place your hand in his, and allow him to guide you, equip you, and empower you for whatever stands in your way.

God loves to take the very circumstance that seemed insurmountable and use it to reveal to you the reality of his power and love. He loves to take the walls of Jericho that seem to stand between you and your dreams and cast down the enemy that you couldn't defeat on your own.

Psalm 32:7 says, *"You are a hiding place for me; you preserve me from trouble; you surround me with shouts of deliverance."* God is surrounding you with his shouts today. The question is, will you have the patience and faith to pause, open your ears, listen, and follow wherever he leads you?

Spend time in prayer allowing God to deliver you, protect you, comfort you, guide you, and give you peace.

GUIDED PRAYER

1. Meditate on God's desire and ability to deliver you from whatever lies before you today.

"When the righteous cry for help, the Lord hears and delivers them out of all their troubles. The Lord is near to the brokenhearted and saves the crushed in spirit." Psalm 34:17-18

"The angel of the Lord encamps around those who fear him, and delivers them." Psalm 34:7

"You are a hiding place for me; you preserve me from trouble; you surround me with shouts of deliverance." Psalm 32:7

2. Reflect on your own life. Where do you need deliverance today? Ask the Spirit to give you revelation about an area from which he wants to deliver you.

3. Spend time in God's presence opening your ears to hear all that he would speak to you. Ask God to deliver you. Pray boldly that your heavenly Father would come through for you in mighty and miraculous ways.

Keep your eyes open today to take notice of all the different ways God answers your prayer. James 1:17 says, *"Every good gift and every perfect gift is from above, coming down from the Father of lights with whom there is no variation or shadow due to change."* God will deliver you because he loves you, and his nature does not change. If he delivered Lazarus, the Israelites, David, and Daniel, he will deliver you. Have confidence in the love and power of your heavenly Father today.

Extended Reading: Psalm 34

DEVOTIONAL

Peace is a commodity that can only be found with time spent seeking the face of God. The world can't offer us peace because it has nothing in which to place its hope, trust, and security. Kingdoms come and go. Leaders move in and out of power. What societies value changes like the passing of the tides. Our only constant is God. He has been, is, and forever will be the Creator, Sustainer, and Lord of all. All authority has been given to him. He governs the change of seasons. He thwarts the plans of our enemy. And he longs to offer total and sustained peace to all who place their hope and trust in him.

Isaiah 26:3 says, *"You keep him in perfect peace whose mind is stayed on you, because he trusts in you."* Our God has peace in store for us in every situation if we will choose to keep our mind stayed on him and trust him. The world says that peace can only come when you've worked your fingers to the bone and have finally attained all you want. You can only have peace when you have enough money, friends, the right job, or the right spouse. You can only have peace if friends, family, and bosses like you. God's way is to draw you into himself and offer you peace in the midst of your circumstances. He doesn't want you to wait until everything gets worked out before you can have rest—he's offering you rest right now.

Psalm 23 says, *"The Lord is my shepherd; I shall not want. He makes me lie down in green pastures. He leads me beside still waters. He restores my soul . . . . You prepare a table before me in the presence of my enemies; you anoint my head with oil; my cup overflows"* (Psalm 23:1-3, 5). God longs to prepare a table for you in the midst of whatever trouble surrounds you. He is calling you to keep your mind stayed on him no matter what lies before you. And he is asking you to seek his face and find your rest in him rather than toiling and striving for circumstantial peace.

Romans 8:6 says, *"To set the mind on the Spirit is life and peace."* It's by the Spirit alone that you will find life and peace. Stop looking for your fulfillment in the things of the world. Stop asking the world to offer you what it never had to begin with. Look toward your heavenly Father for the peace that surpasses all understanding. May you be filled with rest and peace today as you spend time in prayer seeking the face of God.

GUIDED PRAYER

1. Meditate on the truth that God is your sole source of peace and rest. Allow God's word to mold and shape your perspective.

"The Lord is my shepherd; I shall not want. He makes me lie down in green pastures. He leads me beside still waters. He restores my soul." Psalm 23:1-3

"To set the mind on the Spirit is life and peace." Romans 8:6

"You keep him in perfect peace whose mind is stayed on you, because he trusts in you." Isaiah 26:3

2. Where have you been running to for peace? Have you had much peace and rest in your life lately? Acknowledging your past pursuits will help you make present changes.

"Trust in the Lord with all your heart, and do not lean on your own understanding. In all your ways acknowledge him, and he will make your paths straight." Proverbs 3:5-6

3. Seek the peace that comes from placing your hope and trust in God alone. Ask the Spirit to fill you with peace in the midst of your circumstances. Let your requests be known to God, and receive the peace that comes from casting your burdens on the loving and capable shoulders of your heavenly Father.

"The Lord is at hand; do not be anxious about anything, but in everything by prayer and supplication with thanksgiving let your requests be made known to God. And the peace of God, which surpasses all understanding, will guard your hearts and your minds in Christ Jesus." Philippians 4:5-7

You will be robbed of peace as soon as you turn your trust away from God and begin to live in your own strength. The only source of consistent peace is keeping your mind stayed on God. You can trust in the reality of God's desire and ability to help you. You can wait on him if he tells you to wait. You can move when he tells you to move. Offer your understanding, actions, and emotions to him, and allow him to be Lord over them all today.

Extended Reading: Psalm 23

The Lord Gives Contentment

DEVOTIONAL

In Philippians 4, Paul describes what he calls *"the secret"* to contentment. Scripture says, *"Not that I am speaking of being in need, for I have learned in whatever situation I am to be content. I know how to be brought low, and I know how to abound. In any and every circumstance, I*

*"The fear of the Lord leads to life,
and whoever has it rests satisfied."*

PROVERBS 19:23

have learned the secret of facing plenty and hunger, abundance and need. I can do all things through him who strengthens me" (Philippians 4:11-13).

Similarly Hebrews 13:5 says, *"Keep your life free from love of money, and be content with what you have, for he has said, 'I will never leave you nor forsake you.'"* Imagine a life of total contentment regardless of your possessions or status. Imagine the peace, joy, and strength you would find in this kind of freedom Paul experienced from the ways of the world. The question before you today is this: what is keeping you from living your life consistently and completely content?

Scripture is clear that true contentment transcends circumstances. True contentment is found apart from abundant provision. God longs to draw you into a lifestyle of situational transcendence. He longs to provide contentment for you on every level, but it will take surrendering your system of values and pursuits to experience the satisfaction of God's perfect perspective. Contentment comes solely through a lifestyle of surrender.

The truth is, we consistently believe a lie that the world can offer us true contentment. We believe that the next purchase, friend, job, or hobby will satisfy foundational needs that can only find their fulfillment in God. We reach out to the world for help as if the world wasn't in immense need already.

Matthew 6:21 says, *"For where your treasure is, there your heart will be also."* If your value lies in possessions and status, they will own you rather you owning them. If you search after the opinion of man above God's, your contentment will come and go with the fleeting whims of those around you. But if you place your treasure with your heavenly Father, your heart will find its home in the loving arms of God.

If you will find the courage to surrender possessions, family, friends, jobs, and status today, you will find wonderful strength and contentment that transcends this world and finds its source in God alone. Spend time in prayer cutting your emotional ties to the world and placing your hope and trust in your heavenly Father alone.

127

GUIDED PRAYER

1. Meditate on God's desire to bring you contentment that transcends your circumstances.

"The fear of the Lord leads to life, and whoever has it rests satisfied." Proverbs 19:23

2. Where have you been finding your contentment? What have you been seeking after to satisfy your emotional needs? Where have you placed your treasure?

"For where your treasure is, there your heart will be also." Matthew 6:21

"Not that I am speaking of being in need, for I have learned in whatever situation I am to be content. I know how to be brought low, and I know how to abound. In any and every circumstance, I have learned the secret of facing plenty and hunger, abundance and need. I can do all things through him who strengthens me." Philippians 4:11-13

3. Repent of any area in which you have been pursuing the ways of the world, and ask the Holy Spirit to help you value what he values. Ask him how he feels about your possessions and to give you the courage to give away or sell anything that is keeping you from reaching contentment. All that God would lead you to do is perfect and absolutely for your best interest.

"Keep your life free from love of money, and be content with what you have, for he has said, 'I will never leave you nor forsake you.'" Hebrews 13:5

When it comes down to it, what's more valuable than contentment, peace, joy, fulfillment, and love? What possession, friend, job, or status is of greater value than what God has to offer us? The world seeks contentment from avenues which only ever lead to greater need. God has placed before you the avenue of surrender and promised an unconditional and limitless supply of contentment if you will simply take his hand and trust and follow him. May you gain the perfect perspective of your heavenly Father today and pursue the contentment that comes from him alone.

Extended Reading: Matthew 6

The Lord Gives Direction

DAY 26

DEVOTIONAL

Isaiah 48:17-18 offers a hopeful yet heart-wrenching promise of God. Scripture says, *"I am the Lord your God, who teaches you to profit, who leads you in the way you should go. Oh that you had paid attention to my commandments! Then your peace would have been like a river, and your righteousness like the waves of the sea."* What would it be like to experience peace like a river? What would it feel like to float on a continual stream of rest and contentment? How would past circumstances have turned out differently if only we would have listened to the commandments of God? Isaiah makes it clear that a lifestyle of peace and righteousness is readily available to us if we will simply follow the Lord our God *"who leads [us] in the*

way [we] should go." Let's open our hearts and minds to the Spirit of the living God today and ask him to mold and shape us into followers of his direction.

Psalm 32:8-9 says, *"I will instruct you and teach you in the way you should go; I will counsel you with my eye upon you. Be not like a horse or a mule, without understanding, which must be curbed with bit and bridle, or it will not stay near you."* The Lord is faithful to give direction. Psalm 119:105 says, *"Your word is a lamp to my feet and a light to my path."* God's word illuminates the ways in which we should go physically, emotionally, and mentally. His word is designed to influence the ways we think, feel, and act. If we will

> *"The steps of a man are established by the Lord, when he delights in his way."*

PSALM 37:23

choose to follow the direction offered to us in Scripture, we will discover a wellspring of peace and righteousness that completely drenches every part of our hearts with passion and purpose.

Scripture is also clear that God continues to speak to us and offer us direction straight from his voice. John 10:27 says, *"My sheep hear my voice, and I know them, and they follow me."* All throughout the New Testament we see God's people living and working by the direct word of the Lord. The Holy Spirit loves to speak to us and give us knowledge of his plans for us. Our job is to keep our ears open to him and to respond anytime he offers us direction. He longs to

lead us daily into the incredible plans he has for us. He longs to direct us into abundant peace, joy, and purpose. As his sheep we must acknowledge the leadership of our Shepherd and trust in his guidance.

What situation lies before you today in which you need the direction of your all-knowing, loving heavenly Father? Where do you need peace and righteousness today? Where do you need your path illuminated? Dive into the word and God's heart under the guidance of the Holy Spirit, and search out his commandment for your life. Tune your ears to the frequency of God's Spirit and listen to whatever he would say to you. May you discover the direction you need today as you pray.

GUIDED PRAYER

1. Meditate on God's desire and ability to offer you direction through his word and voice.

"Your word is a lamp to my feet and a light to my path." Psalm 119:105

"The steps of a man are established by the Lord, when he delights in his way." Psalm 37:23

"My sheep hear my voice, and I know them, and they follow me." John 10:27

2. Where do you need God's direction today?
Where do you need the peace that comes from knowing God's will and desire for you?

"Thus says the Lord, your Redeemer, the Holy One of Israel: 'I am the Lord your God, who teaches you to profit, who leads you in the way you should go. Oh that you had paid attention to my commandments! Then your peace would have been like a river, and your righteousness like the waves of the sea.'" Isaiah 48:17-18

3. Ask the Spirit to direct you right now, and dive into what God's word says about your circumstances. Trust that God will speak to you perfectly because he loves you. He will make his will known to you if you ask him.

"I will instruct you and teach you in the way you should go; I will counsel you with my eye upon you. Be not like a horse or a mule, without understanding, which must be curbed with bit and bridle, or it will not stay near you." Psalm 32:8-9

God never desires to send you out into this world on your own. He longs to establish you as a good follower of his direction. He longs to teach you how to live your life under the guidance of the Spirit and the word. Spend time receiving fresh revelation on what it looks like to follow your heavenly Father and receive his will. Ask him to guide you throughout your day today and teach you how to be a good follower.

Extended Reading: Psalm 32

God the Giver of Strength

DEVOTIONAL

The story of God's people is one of God's strength covering our weakness. Our heavenly Father takes our problems, sins, fears, and feebleness and uses them as opportunities to demonstrate the overwhelming power of his love. He takes those the world deems to be the weakest and uses them to accomplish incredible, powerful works. Isaiah 40:28-31 says:

"My flesh and my heart may fail, but God is the strength of my heart and my portion forever."

PSALM 73:26

135

Have you not known? Have you not heard? The Lord is the everlasting God, the Creator of the ends of the earth. He does not faint or grow weary; his understanding is unsearchable. He gives power to the faint, and to him who has no might he increases strength. Even youths shall faint and be weary, and young men shall fall exhausted; but they who wait for the Lord shall renew their strength; they shall mount up with wings like eagles; they shall run and not be weary; they shall walk and not faint.

Our God knows our frame. He knows that our bodies have come from dust and will one day return to their original form. He knows that without his help we accomplish nothing. But Paul's declaration in Philippians 4:13 is just as true for you and me as it was for him: *"I can do all things through him who strengthens me."* We can do all things through the anointing and power of our heavenly Father. We can tackle any obstacle that stands in our way because our God is perfectly strong in our weakness.

Where do you need the strength of God today? Where do you feel weak, powerless, or weary? Where do you need to run but only feel exhausted? Your lot is not to go through life living solely by your own power. You've been given a new identity as a son or daughter of the Most High God who desperately wants to clothe you with strength and teach you how to use the authority given to you by Jesus.

In God you can defeat the powers of sin and darkness that have held you back. In God you can accomplish the tasks set before you with joy, energy, and strength. And in God you can love and be loved to such a capacity that your very attitude, outlook, and emotions transform into reflections of your heavenly Father's.

Spend time in prayer receiving the strength that comes from God alone. Allow him to fill you with fresh vision and align your perspective with his.

GUIDED PRAYER

1. Meditate on God's desire to fill you with strength.

"Fear not, for I am with you; be not dismayed, for I am your God; I will strengthen you, I will help you, I will uphold you with my righteous right hand." Isaiah 41:10

"Have you not known? Have you not heard? The Lord is the everlasting God, the Creator of the ends of the earth. He does not faint or grow weary; his understanding is unsearchable. He gives power to the faint, and to him who has no might he increases strength. Even youths shall faint and be weary, and young men shall fall exhausted; but they who wait for the Lord shall renew their strength; they shall mount up with wings like eagles; they shall run and not be weary; they shall walk and not faint." Isaiah 40:28-31

2. Where do you need God's strength today?

Where do you feel weakest? Where do you need his power and anointing?

3. Ask God to fill you with the power of the Holy Spirit.

Ask him to make his strength known to you. Allow your perspective and outlook to shift in light of God's power and love.

"My flesh and my heart may fail, but God is the strength of my heart and my portion forever." Psalm 73:26

"It is God who arms me with strength and keeps my way secure. He makes my feet like the feet of a deer; he causes me to stand on the heights." 2 Samuel 22:33-34 NIV

"I can do all things through him who strengthens me." Philippians 4:13

We are never meant to do life on our own. We are designed to be in connection to the strength of our heavenly Father in every situation, relationship, job, and trial. God longs to fill us with strength to accomplish the good work laid before us. He longs to make us strong in him. Don't go throughout your day in your own strength. Instead, seek out the hand of your heavenly Father and allow him to help you today.

Extended Reading: Psalm 73

God the Giver of Courage

DEVOTIONAL

Your portion as a child of the Most High God is a life filled with bravery and courage. The Lord desires to take what brings you fear and force it out with an infilling of courage rooted in the truth of his word for you. Open your heart and mind today to receive healing and transformation in the areas of fear, insecurity, and doubt. Allow God to come in and do a mighty work that frees you to live with joy, security, and courage.

"Wait for the Lord; be strong, and let your heart take courage; wait for the Lord!"

PSALM 27:14

In God we have a constant source of courage. Isaiah 43:2-3 says, *"When you pass through the waters, I will be with you; and through the rivers, they shall not overwhelm you; when you walk through fire you shall not be burned, and the flame shall not consume you. For I am the Lord your God, the Holy One of Israel, your Savior."* Your heavenly Father is always with you. He will never leave nor forsake you. And in every situation, trial, and problem, he has a perfect plan to guide you into a lifestyle of strength, courage, and peace.

1 John 4:18 says, *"There is no fear in love, but perfect love casts out fear."* God's love has the power to drive out every source of insecurity and fear that plagues you. His loving presence fills every crevasse of our hearts, satiating and healing all our longings and wounds. His Spirit speaks truth where lies and wrong perspectives have led us away from life as sons and daughters of the King. And his word remains a constant reminder of the power and freedom available to those who trust in their God over their own feelings of weakness and insecurity.

Romans 8:15 says, *"For you did not receive the spirit of slavery to fall back into fear, but you have received the Spirit of adoption as sons, by whom we cry, 'Abba! Father!'"* The death of Christ brought you a new Spirit. And it's in that Spirit that we are now filled with new identity, new purpose, and new perspective. When you find yourself in a situation that would normally fill you with fear, call upon the power of the Spirit and ask him to fill you with fresh vision, strength, and courage. Renew your mind to the truth that you are no longer a citizen of this world and are not subject to the emotions, fears, doubts, and insecurities that come with it. You are now a child of the omnipotent, omnipresent, and fully loving Creator of all.

David wrote in Psalm 34:4, *"I sought the Lord, and he answered me and delivered me from all my fears."* May you seek the face of your heavenly Father today, press into the heart of God for all the healing and deliverance he longs to give you, and find yourself freed from the fears and insecurities that have held you back for far too long.

GUIDED PRAYER

1. Meditate on your new portion as a child of God. Renew your mind to the truth of the courage and security available to you in Christ.

"For God gave us a spirit not of fear but of power and love and self-control." 2 Timothy 1:7

"For you did not receive the spirit of slavery to fall back into fear, but you have received the Spirit of adoption as sons, by whom we cry, 'Abba! Father!'" Romans 8:15

2. Reflect on your life. What situations fill you with insecurity and fear? What person, past wound, or lie has left you crippled or afraid? Where do you need the courage and bravery of God today?

3. Rest in the presence of God, and allow his love to cast out fear and fill you with courage and truth.

"There is no fear in love, but perfect love casts out fear." 1 John 4:18

"When you pass through the waters, I will be with you; and through the rivers, they shall not overwhelm you; when you walk through fire you shall not be burned, and the flame shall not consume you. For I am the Lord your God, the Holy One of Israel, your Savior." Isaiah 43:2-3

"I sought the Lord, and he answered me and delivered me from all my fears." Psalm 34:4

May you have fresh vision for the abundant courage available to you in God. May you pursue wholeheartedly the transformation God longs to work in you. Don't be content with less than God desires for you. Instead, passionately seek out the life Christ died to give you. Find courage, hope, and fulfillment today in the nearness and love of your heavenly Father.

Extended Reading: 1 John 4

The father heart of God

*"One God and Father of all,
who is over all and through
all and in all." Ephesians 4:6*

WEEKLY OVERVIEW

There is no better father than Creator God. He formed us and knows us. He provides for us, loves us unconditionally, and longs for real, life-giving relationship with us. He runs out to meet us in our sin, clothes us with new identity, and restores to us the abundant life he has always planned for us. As we spend time looking at the father heart of God, may a fresh revelation of his love for you guide you into greater depths of relationship with your heavenly Father.

An Unconditional Love

DEVOTIONAL

In Brennan Manning's book, *Abba's Child: The Cry of the Heart for Intimate Belonging,* he writes,

"But we cannot assume that [God] feels about us the way we feel about ourselves—unless we love ourselves compassionately, intensely, and freely. In human form Jesus revealed to us what God is like. He exposed our projections for the idolatry that they are and gave us the way to become free of them. It takes a profound conversion to accept that God is relentlessly tender and compassionate toward us just as we are—not in spite of our sins and faults (that would not be total acceptance), but with them. Though God does not condone or sanction evil, He does not withhold his love because there is evil in us."

May we experience the freedom that comes with a true revelation of God's unceasing love for us.

"There is no fear in love, but perfect love casts out fear. For fear has to do with punishment, and whoever fears has not been perfected in love."

1 JOHN 4:18

God loves you with an unconditional love. To know God is to know love in its truest form, because he is love. Love isn't just something he gives. It isn't just something that he feels. It is who he is. God's love for you is limitless and has the power to set you free from every wound, thought, sin, and broken relationship that causes you to live anything less than a joyful and content life.

Romans 5:8 says, *"But God shows his love for us in that while we were still sinners, Christ died for us."* Really take a minute today and allow the truth of God's word to settle into your heart. While you were still a sinner, Christ gave his life that you might live. God demonstrated the depth of his love for you by sending Jesus to die while you were still a slave to sin. At your lowest point, God loved you with an everlasting love. There is no need to cleanse or fix yourself before you run into the arms of God. There is no need to fake happiness or holiness with your heavenly Father. God loved you prior to clothing you with Christ. He will love you in the midst of every mistake you make, and he will love you whether or not you ever love him back. His wrath was satisfied with the death of Jesus so that you could come to him just as you are and simply experience his love.

Titus 3:4-5 says, *"But when the goodness and loving kindness of God our Savior appeared, he saved us, not because of works done by us in righteousness, but according to his own mercy, by the washing of regeneration and renewal of the Holy Spirit."* Take time in guided prayer to allow the Holy Spirit to wash you with regeneration and renewal. Allow God to cast out any fear or reservation that is keeping you from experiencing the fullness of his love. Allow him to establish a new foundation of grace on which you live with unshakable joy and security in the affections of your heavenly Father.

GUIDED PRAYER

1. Meditate on the depth of God's love for you. Allow the truth of his grace and mercy to settle in and change your perspectives.

"But God shows his love for us in that while we were still sinners, Christ died for us." Romans 5:8

"Can a woman forget her nursing child, that she should have no compassion on the son of her womb? Even these may forget, yet I will not forget you. Behold, I have engraved you on the palms of my hands; your walls are continually before me." Isaiah 49:15-16

2. What keeps you from experiencing God's love? What thought or wound holds you back from spending more time with your heavenly Father?

"There is no fear in love, but perfect love casts out fear. For fear has to do with punishment, and whoever fears has not been perfected in love." 1 John 4:18

3. Allow God's love to renew within you a longing to spend more time with him. Rest in his presence.

Receive a fresh revelation of his goodness. Spend time with your heavenly Father just letting him love you.

"The Lord appeared to him from far away. I have loved you with an everlasting love; therefore I have continued my faithfulness to you." Jeremiah 31:3

"See what kind of love the Father has given to us, that we should be called children of God; and so we are." 1 John 3:1

It's vital that as believers we are constantly checking the status of our mental and emotional health. A single lie planted in our mind has the power to steer us away from experiencing the fullness of God's love. If you are having a hard time pursuing relationship with God, take some time to find out why. If you can't seem to find joy, take time to do a mental and emotional inventory. May you experience freedom from whatever thought, belief, past or present event, worry, or doubt that is keeping you from the abundant life Jesus came to give you.

Extended Reading: Romans 5

The Patient Passion of God

DAY 30

DEVOTIONAL

There is no virtue more calming than patience. A peaceful lifestyle begins with patience. When birthed by a heavenly perspective, patience can transform even the most stressful places of one's heart into calm streams of joy and abundant life.

"The Lord is not slow to fulfill his promise as some count slowness, but is patient toward you, not wishing that any should perish, but that all should reach repentance."

2 PETER 3:9

Our heavenly Father perfectly models a patient heart. 2 Peter 3:8-9 says, *"But do not overlook this one fact, beloved, that with the Lord one day is as a thousand years, and a thousand years as one day. The Lord is not slow to fulfill his promise as some count slowness, but is patient toward you, not wishing that any should perish, but that all should reach repentance."* God's perspective and overwhelming love for us fill his heart with incredible patience.

Think for a second about all the atrocities, perversions, sin, and depravity God witnesses on a continual basis. He watches in pain as humanity kills, steals, lies, and cheats. He watches as those he most cares for throw away his perfect plans for cheap imitations that only cause heartache and pain. But God in his patient mercy waits to return and bring about the complete restoration of creation that all might reach repentance. God is patient because he is love.

God is not only patient in regard to the second coming of Jesus. He is wholly patient with you in regards to your sanctification and relationship with him and others. He beckons you moment by moment, whispering to your heart about the great plans he has for your life. He waits patiently as he transforms you into a reflection of Jesus by filling you with his abundant love. He knows your frame. He knows the wounds the world has caused. And he is patient with you.

Take time this morning to slow down and take a deep breath. Carve out some space in the busyness of your life and rest in response to God's patience. God isn't in a rush with his plans for you. He isn't in a rush to fix you. He simply longs for you to take some time and be with him. He wants to overwhelm you with his patient love that you might live free from the burdens and cares of this rushed, stressed world.

Psalm 103:8 says, *"The Lord is merciful and gracious, slow to anger and abounding in steadfast love."* May you encounter the patient, merciful, gracious, peaceful, and loving presence of your heavenly Father as you enter into guided prayer.

GUIDED PRAYER

1. Meditate on the patient heart of your heavenly Father. Ask the Holy Spirit to give you a revelation of how patient God is with you as you mull over his words.

"The Lord is not slow to fulfill his promise as some count slowness, but is patient toward you, not wishing that any should perish, but that all should reach repentance." 2 Peter 3:9

"Have you not known? Have you not heard? The Lord is the everlasting God, the Creator of the ends of the earth. He does not faint or grow weary; his understanding is unsearchable." Isaiah 40:28

"The Lord is merciful and gracious, slow to anger and abounding in steadfast love." Psalm 103:8

2. Where do you need an increase of patience today? What burden or care doesn't line up with the heavenly perspective of patience?

3. Ask the Holy Spirit to help you be patient like your heavenly Father. Ask him to give you a heavenly perspective about your life so that you can cast off stress and burden. Pursue patience and passion for all God has given you.

Oftentimes we believe patience and passion can't be connected. We see examples of those who achieved so much seemingly out of a lack of patience and believe that we need to be as rushed and stressed as they were in order to have a meaningful life. That is not the case with God. God's timing is perfect. His will can be known. If you will trust the patient heart of your heavenly Father and live as he directs, you will achieve the purpose for which you have been called. Seek the face of your heavenly Father today for wisdom and direction. Pursue passion with patience. And discover the wealth of joy and peace that comes from having patience for yourself and others as your heavenly Father does.

Extended Reading: Psalm 103

155

God is Present

DAY 31

DEVOTIONAL

If there's one truth that has the power to guide you into the fullness of life available to you in Christ, it's that God is present. Psalm 139:7-10 says,

Where shall I go from your Spirit? Or where shall I flee from your presence? If I ascend to heaven, you are there! If I make my bed in Sheol, you are there! If I take the wings of the morning and dwell in the uttermost parts of the sea, even there your hand shall lead me, and your right hand shall hold me.

No matter where you go, no matter what you do, God is with you. And he isn't just with you in an abstract sense, he is available for you to tangibly and powerfully experience. Psalm 23:4 says, *"Even though I walk through the valley of the shadow of death, I will fear no evil, for you are with me; your rod and your staff, they comfort me."* In the presence of the Lord there is fullness of comfort. Throughout every season of your life, he is there ready to empower you, encourage you, strengthen you, and love you. He longs to meet you where you're at and provide all the guidance, love, comfort, and fatherly encouragement you need.

You see, when God meets with us he both satisfies our emotions and transforms us. He heals our hearts and empowers us to live the life he has planned for us. As our Father, he not only comforts us when we

> *"Be strong and courageous. Do not fear or be in dread of them, for it is the Lord your God who goes with you. He will not leave you or forsake you."*
>
> **DEUTERONOMY 31:6**

need him, but guides and helps us through the various seasons of life. God is present not only to love you emotionally, but practically as well.

Isaiah 41:10 says, *"Fear not, for I am with you; be not dismayed, for I am your God; I will strengthen you, I will help you, I will uphold you with my righteous right hand."* As a father teaches his son or daughter how to walk by upholding them, your God longs to uphold you through whatever decision, trial, season, or pain you are presently experiencing. He is not a distant God who just gives his children rules and tells them to go through life on their own. He is not a far-off Creator who leaves his creation to its own devices. He is

working presently in our midst to shepherd us toward the fullness of life Jesus died to give us. There is no more present, loving, or powerful father than our God. There is no greater helper than the Holy Spirit who dwells within us. And there is no greater life than one lived in constant communion with our Creator.

Whatever season you find yourself in today, press into the heart of your heavenly Father. As you enter into guided prayer, allow God to fill you, satisfy you, comfort you, and love you. Allow him to shepherd you, empower you, uphold you, and encourage you. Experience the nearness of your heavenly Father and walk today in constant communion with your God who is present.

GUIDED PRAYER

1. Meditate on the fact that God is present. Allow Scripture to fill you with the faith to encounter your heavenly Father today.

"'Am I a God at hand, declares the Lord, and not a God far away? Can a man hide himself in secret places so that I cannot see him?' declares the Lord. 'Do I not fill heaven and earth?' declares the Lord." Jeremiah 23:23-24

"The Lord has taken away the judgments against you; he has cleared away your enemies. The King of Israel, the Lord, is in your midst; you shall never again fear evil." Zephaniah 3:15

"Be strong and courageous. Do not fear or be in dread of them, for it is the Lord your God who goes with you. He will not leave you or forsake you." Deuteronomy 31:6

2. Where do you need God to be present in your life? Where do you need his encouragement, love, guidance, and empowerment?

3. Ask God to make his presence known to you. Ask him to fill you with his love and nearness. Rest in his presence and allow him to love you and speak to you.

"My sheep hear my voice, and I know them, and they follow me. I give them eternal life, and they will never perish, and no one will snatch them out of my hand." John 10:27-28

"So we have come to know and to believe the love that God has for us. God is love, and whoever abides in love abides in God, and God abides in him." 1 John 4:16

A vital part of Christian spirituality is making time to simply fellowship with God. Resting in the presence of the Lord puts all of life in perspective. It places God at a higher value than whatever else we could spend our time pursuing. It empowers us to live peacefully and purposefully. And it lays a foundation of God's love on which we can live out the calling given to us by our heavenly Father. Take time throughout your day to receive God's presence. Allow him to flood wherever you are with his love and encouragement. May your day be transformed by the nearness of God.

Extended Reading: Psalm 139

God is Our Provider

DAY 32

DEVOTIONAL

In Matthew 6:25-33 Jesus says,

Therefore I tell you, do not be anxious about your life, what you will eat or what you will drink, nor about your body, what you will put on. Is not life more than food, and the body more than clothing? Look at the birds of the air: they neither sow nor reap nor gather into barns, and yet your heavenly Father feeds them. Are you not of more value than they? And which of you by being anxious can add a single hour to his span of life? And why are you anxious about clothing? Consider the lilies of the field, how they grow: they neither toil nor spin,

*"And my God will supply every need of yours
according to his riches in glory in Christ Jesus."*

PHILIPPIANS 4:19

yet I tell you, even Solomon in all his glory was not arrayed like one of these. But if God so clothes the grass of the field, which today is alive and tomorrow is thrown into the oven, will he not much more clothe you, O you of little faith? Therefore do not be anxious, saying, 'What shall we eat?' or 'What shall we drink?' or 'What shall we wear?' For the Gentiles seek after all these things, and your heavenly Father knows that you need them all. But seek first the kingdom of God and his righteousness, and all these things will be added to you.

Your heavenly Father is the Great Provider for all the earth. He gives rain when the earth needs refreshment. He calls the sun from its hiding when the earth needs warmth. He gives to the animals their food, the flowers their beauty, the birds their shelter, and you and me everything we need.

We worship a God who is both loving and powerful. He is both omnipotent and omnipresent. He is both good and able. If he were not, we would be forced to fend for ourselves, striving for that which he has promised to provide. If he were only good, we would not be assured of the provision his power provides.

And if he were only able, we would fear for a lack of his desire to provide. But God is our heavenly Father who both knows what we need and longs to provide for us in exceeding measures. He is our Creator and Sustainer, Lord of all and Lord in all.

So why do you fear for your needs? Why do you stress over the foundational cares of this life while your heavenly Father is seated on his throne? The truth is that until we experience for ourselves both the goodness and power of our heavenly Father, the truth of his provision will only ever feel like a heady, theological principle. Until we experience firsthand the character and provision of our God, fear will remain.

1 John 4:18 says, *"There is no fear in love, but perfect love casts out fear. For fear has to do with punishment, and whoever fears has not been perfected in love."* God longs to perfect you in his love today. He longs to guide you into an encounter with his goodness and power. He longs to establish a foundation of his faithfulness by which you can live in faith. May you have a transformative encounter with the Holy Spirit today that frees you from fear and striving as you enter into guided prayer.

161

GUIDED PRAYER

1. Meditate on God's promises of provision. Allow Scripture to renew your mind and transform the way you act, think, and feel.

"Ask, and it will be given to you; seek, and you will find; knock, and it will be opened to you. For everyone who asks receives, and the one who seeks finds, and to the one who knocks it will be opened. Or which one of you, if his son asks him for bread, will give him a stone? Or if he asks for a fish, will give him a serpent? If you then, who are evil, know how to give good gifts to your children, how much more will your Father who is in heaven give good things to those who ask him!" Matthew 7:7-11

"And my God will supply every need of yours according to his riches in glory in Christ Jesus." Philippians 4:19

2. Where do you have fear in regards to provision? Where are you striving for what God has already promised to provide? Where does God want to bring peace into your life today?

3. Take time to allow God to reveal his goodness and power. Ask the Holy Spirit to guide you into an encounter with all that God is. Allow Scripture to speak to your circumstances so that you might live today in line with God's promises.

No matter how old we get, God will still be our Father. We never have to go through a season apart from his perfect provision. We never have to step outside of his leadership and love. He will always be our Good Shepherd. He will always be our Sustainer. And he will always be our heavenly Father who provides. Never doubt the goodness and power of your God. Rest in his promises. And continue to grow in your knowledge of who he is by resting in his presence. May you experience today the abundant provision of your loving, heavenly Father.

Extended Reading: Philippians 4

God Encourages Us

DEVOTIONAL

Our God is the great encourager. He takes the weak
and makes them strong. He takes the hopeless and
transforms them into beacons of eternal salvation.
He takes the broken and heals them with his
love. And he takes the doubting and fills them
with powerful encouragement from on high.

"What then shall we say to these things?
If God is for us, who can be against us?"

ROMANS 8:31

Our heavenly Father longs to give you confidence today. He longs to encourage you to accomplish the incredible calling for which you were created. As we look today at a powerful story of God's encouragement, may your heart be filled with a longing and passion to seek out the entirety of God's perfect plans for you. Judges 6:12-18 says,

And the angel of the Lord appeared to [Gideon] and said to him, "The Lord is with you, O mighty man of valor." And Gideon said to him, "Please, sir, if the Lord is with us, why then has all this happened to us? And where are all his wonderful deeds that our fathers recounted to us, saying, 'Did not the Lord bring us up from Egypt?' But now the Lord has forsaken us and given us into the hand of Midian." And the Lord turned to him and said, "Go in this might of yours and save Israel from the hand of Midian; do not I send you?" And he said to him, "Please, Lord, how can I save Israel? Behold, my clan is the weakest in Manasseh, and I am the least in my father's house." And the Lord said to him, "But I will be with you, and you shall strike the Midianites as one man." And he said to him, "If now I have found favor in your eyes, then show me a sign that it is you who speak with me. Please do not depart from here until I come to you and bring out my present and set it before you." And he said, "I will stay till you return."

God calls Gideon a mighty man of valor prior to any mighty actions Gideon had done. He commands Gideon to go out in the might to which he was called and accomplish the very work for which he was created. And when Gideon responds by asking God for a sign, God obliges him and remains with grace and mercy.

God is calling you to a life of eternal significance. He's calling you to a life that matters. There is no weak tool in the hands of God. And there is no small calling in his perfect plans. You were created to live a life that changes the world. You were created for a destiny that draws the lost back into the fold of our heavenly Father. But in order to accomplish the life to which you were called you will need courage. You will need time spent in God's presence being filled with his encouragement.

God is calling you a mighty man or woman of valor. He is speaking strength over you. He is near to you, ready and able to empower you. Take time in guided prayer to hear the voice of your heavenly Father. Allow his Spirit to speak to your spirit. Allow him to encourage you in his love. And follow his voice in faith that you might be used in greater ways than you could ever imagine.

165

GUIDED PRAYER

1. Meditate on God's desire to encourage you. Allow Scripture to fill you with the truth about the life God intends for you.

"But you are a chosen race, a royal priesthood, a holy nation, a people for his own possession, that you may proclaim the excellencies of him who called you out of darkness into his marvelous light." 1 Peter 2:9

"But the saints of the Most High shall receive the kingdom and possess the kingdom forever, forever and ever." Daniel 7:18

"For I know the plans I have for you, declares the Lord, plans for welfare and not for evil, to give you a future and a hope." Jeremiah 29:11

2. Where do you need courage to pursue the life to which God has called you? What is God calling you to today that seems impossible? What has God spoken over you in the past that fear has crippled you from pursuing?

3. Allow God to fill you with confidence. Open your heart to him and ask him to empower you and fill you with his love. Rest in his nearness. Allow Scripture to fill you with faith to pursue to the fullest whatever God asks you to do.

"Wait for the Lord; be strong, and let your heart take courage; wait for the Lord!" Psalm 27:14

"What then shall we say to these things? If God is for us, who can be against us?" Romans 8:31

"For we are his workmanship, created in Christ Jesus for good works, which God prepared beforehand, that we should walk in them." Ephesians 2:10

Don't settle for a life of mediocrity today. God has a plan and purpose for everything you do. He longs to turn your relationships, job, finances, and passions into good works of eternal significance. His calling will satisfy your heart like nothing else. And the empowerment of his Spirit for his plans will transform you into a passionate, effective, and loving man or woman of valor. May you pursue wholeheartedly the life to which you have been called by your loving heavenly Father.

Extended Reading: Judges 6

God Disciplines Us in Love

DAY 34

DEVOTIONAL

Our world despises discipline. We view correction as an attempt to keep us from doing what we really want rather than an act of love to guide us toward a more abundant life. If we are ever going to live the incredible life God longs to give us, we need renewal in the area of discipline. We must allow God to correct and shape us as the potter molds the clay so that we can live the life to which we have been called.

"My son, do not regard lightly the discipline of the Lord, nor be weary when reproved by him. For the Lord disciplines the one he loves, and chastises every son whom he receives."

HEBREWS 12:6

Our heavenly Father never disciplines out of anger or frustration, but only out of love. Hebrews 12:7-14 says,

It is for discipline that you have to endure. God is treating you as sons. For what son is there whom his father does not discipline? If you are left without discipline, in which all have participated, then you are illegitimate children and not sons. Besides this, we have had earthly fathers who disciplined us and we respected them. Shall we not much more be subject to the Father of spirits and live? For they disciplined us for a short time as it seemed best to them, but he disciplines us for our good, that we may share his holiness. For the moment all discipline seems painful rather than pleasant, but later it yields the peaceful fruit of righteousness to those who have been trained by it. Therefore lift your drooping hands and strengthen your weak knees, and make straight paths for your feet, so that what is lame may not be put out of joint but rather be healed. Strive for peace with everyone, and for the holiness without which no one will see the Lord.

God longs to establish a foundation of discipline in your relationship with him because he loves you. It's our pride and lack of revelation that keeps us

from allowing God to correct us. If we truly knew the abundant life available to us on the other side of discipline, we would run to the forming hands of our God rather than hiding from them. If we had revelation on the incredible plans God longs to equip us for, we would yearn for the loving correction of our Father rather than withholding the broken places in our hearts from him.

Your heavenly Father has greater plans than you could ever ask or imagine in store if you will allow him to mold and shape you through discipline. He longs to correct every area of your heart that isn't bearing the fruit of the Spirit or producing abundant life. He longs to provide discipline for your sin so that you can live in the freedom of righteousness.

Open your heart to his loving discipline today. Allow him to mold and fashion you into the likeness of Jesus. Spend time allowing his love to wash you clean and free you from the bonds of sin. May you have a powerful encounter with the loving discipline of your heavenly Father as you enter into guided prayer.

169

GUIDED PRAYER

1. Meditate on the value of being disciplined by your loving heavenly Father. Allow Scripture to change the way you view discipline and correction.

"Whoever spares the rod hates his son, but he who loves him is diligent to discipline him." Proverbs 13:24

"And have you forgotten the exhortation that addresses you as sons? 'My son, do not regard lightly the discipline of the Lord, nor be weary when reproved by him. For the Lord disciplines the one he loves, and chastises every son whom he receives.'" Hebrews 12:5-6

"A wise son hears his father's instruction, but a scoffer does not listen to rebuke." Proverbs 13:1

2. Where do you need to be disciplined today? What part of your life does not line up with God's plans for you? Where does God need to prune you so that you might bear more fruit of the Spirit?

"Blessed is the man whom you discipline, O Lord, and whom you teach out of your law, to give him rest from days of trouble, until a pit is dug for the wicked." Psalm 94:12-13

3. Spend time allowing God to love and correct you. Ask him to prune and teach you. Ask him to guide you into a lifestyle of greater confession, repentance, forgiveness, and healing.

Sometimes the best instruments of correction are fellow believers. Ask the Lord if there is anyone you need to confess your sin to. James 5:16 says, *"Therefore, confess your sins to one another and pray for one another, that you may be healed. The prayer of a righteous person has great power as it is working."* Ask for wisdom from the men and women in your life who are experiencing freedom and abundance in an area in which you have need. May you experience the entire abundant life available to you through the loving discipline of your heavenly Father and the fellow believers he has placed in your midst.

Extended Reading: Hebrews 12

God is a Fun Father

DAY 35

DEVOTIONAL

There is a terrible misconception in the church today that our Father is not a fun God. For most Christians, what they know of God comes through worship services rather than direct encounters with the living God. As the body of Christ, we have not cultivated a culture of restored relationship well. But regardless of faults in the church today, God longs to give you a revelation of how incredibly fun it is to have him as your Father. He longs to guide you into a lifestyle of abundant joy as you grow in your relationship with him.

While God's fun may look different than the world's, every form of fun apart from his is a cheap imitation. We see countless examples in Scripture of God's children experiencing a depth of joy unattainable apart from God. David writes in Psalm 16:11, *"You make known to me the path of life; in your presence there is fullness of joy: at your right hand are pleasures forevermore."* The fullness of fun is found with God because he alone guides us to the path of true life. He alone frees us, heals us, loves us, rejoices over us, has grace for us, and longs to fully satisfy our desires. In John 10:10 Jesus said, *"The thief comes only to steal and kill and destroy. I came that they may have life and have it abundantly."* God longs to lead you to the fullness of life today. He longs to guide you to the riches of his love that you might experience how fun it is to be truly loved by your Creator, Sustainer, and Lord.

Our Father loves parties. He loves to celebrate and have fun with his children. Ecclesiastes 2:24-26 says, *"There is nothing better for a person than that he should eat and drink and find enjoyment in his toil.*

"You have turned for me my mourning into dancing; you have loosed my sackcloth and clothed me with gladness, that my glory may sing your praise and not be silent. O Lord my God, I will give thanks to you forever!"

PSALM 30:11-12

This also, I saw, is from the hand of God, for apart from him who can eat or who can have enjoyment? For to the one who pleases him God has given wisdom and knowledge and joy." Jesus' first miracle was turning water into wine to keep a wedding feast going (John 2:1-11). The Parable of the Prodigal Son in Luke 15 is the story Jesus told of an earthly father and son and a parallel to our relationship with the heavenly Father. When the prodigal son returns home, the father tells his servants, *"Bring quickly the best robe, and put it on him, and put a ring on his hand, and shoes on his feet. And bring the fattened calf and kill it, and let us eat and celebrate. For this my son was dead, and is alive again; he was lost, and is found"* (Luke 15:22-24). While the older son was out in the field, he heard everyone celebrating with music and dancing. He couldn't help but go see what was going on. And

Revelation 19 foretells the great marriage supper of the Lamb where we will celebrate our total and complete union with God, the party to end all parties.

Psalm 30:11-12 says, *"You have turned for me my mourning into dancing; you have loosed my sackcloth and clothed me with gladness, that my glory may sing your praise and not be silent. O Lord my God, I will give thanks to you forever!"* Your heavenly Father longs to lead you to the fullness of fun today. He longs to clothe you with gladness and turn your mourning into dancing. The God you serve is the inventor of fun. He loves to celebrate with his children. He longs to fill your days with that which will satisfy the deepest longings of your heart, including your need for fun. May you encounter the fun heart of your heavenly Father today as you enter into guided prayer.

GUIDED PRAYER

1. Meditate on God's desire to give you a fun life. Allow Scripture to reorient your understanding of what it's like to live life with your heavenly Father.

"You make known to me the path of life; in your presence there is fullness of joy; at your right hand are pleasures forevermore." Psalm 16:11

"You have turned for me my mourning into dancing; you have loosed my sackcloth and clothed me with gladness, that my glory may sing your praise and not be silent. O Lord my God, I will give thanks to you forever!" Psalm 30:11-12

"There is nothing better for a person than that he should eat and drink and find enjoyment in his toil. This also, I saw, is from the hand of God, for apart from him who can eat or who can have enjoyment? For to the one who pleases him God has given wisdom and knowledge and joy." Ecclesiastes 2:24-26

2. Where do you need more fun in your life? Where do you need God to clothe you with gladness? Where do you need to experience the abundant life Jesus died to give you?

3. Ask the Holy Spirit to show you how to have the fullness of fun today. What is he providing for you that you might experience all the joy and celebration available to you? What is keeping you from living a more fun life? He wants to free you today. Spend timing resting in his presence and allow him to do a work in your heart today.

Sometimes we hold to an idea that advancing the kingdom and having fun don't go together. We leave parties and fun to others as we are too busy with more important matters. But why would a nonbeliever want to get to know a boring God? Why would they want to spend time with a group of boring people? As children of God, we have the greatest source of joy available. We should be the happiest, most fun, and most loving people the lost will ever encounter. It's in our joy, love, and fun that we will best advance the kingdom. It's living the abundant life God longs to give us that will encourage others to want to know the God we serve. May you advance the kingdom of your heavenly Father by living today with the fullness of fun.

Extended Reading: Luke 15